Communion

Seán Swayne

Communion

The new Rite of Mass

Veritas Publications Dublin 1974

First published 1974 by
Veritas Publications,
Pranstown House, Booterstown Avenue, Co. Dublin.

Printed and bound in the Republic of Ireland by
Cahill and Co. Limited, Dublin.

Designed by Liam Miller.
Cover by Steven Hope.

Acknowledgements:
The author and publishers are obliged to The Dacre Press,
London, for permission to quote from *The Shape of the Liturgy*
by G. Dix. If any involuntary infringement of copyright has
been committed, sincere apologies are offered; the error will
be rectified in future editions.

NIHIL OBSTAT:
John Whelan, s.t.l.,
Censor deputatus.

IMPRIMI POTEST:
✠Dermot,
Archbishop of Dublin.
4th July, 1974.

ISBN 0–901810–75–4
CAT. NO. 3306.

Contents

Prefatory Note

It is a great pleasure to recommend *Communion* by Father Seán Swayne, Secretary to the Irish Episcopal Commission for Liturgy and energetic organiser of the Liturgy Centre at Mount St Anne's, Portarlington.

There is a general impression about that a good deal of writing on the *Ordo Missae* of 1970 has appeared. As far as the English language is concerned, this is not so and much remains to be done if the riches of the Order are to be appreciated and reduced to practice. For this we need, among other things, books; but they must be well informed and inspired by good pastoral sense. I have no hesitation in saying that this is such a book.

First, it is based on sound scholarship—Father Swayne is a *diplome* of the *Institut Supérieur de Liturgie* of Paris—without which, writing on liturgical matters is nearly always useless. Secondly, the author has the gift of clear exposition that makes the reading of his book a pleasure. To those who teach, whether they are the clergy, religious or the laity, it will be a useful and, one is inclined to say, an indispensable instrument. In addition, Father Swayne's attitude to the *Ordo* is wholly positive. He has seized hold of the meaning of the rite and enables his readers to understand its significance as a whole and in its various parts. His treatment of that difficult part of the Mass, the "presentation of the gifts", is noteworthy.

The celebration of the Mass requires of both priests and people that "full, conscious and active participation" of which the *Constitution on the Liturgy* speaks (14). Such participation demands understanding, but the sort of understanding that is orientated to action, to celebration in fact. It is this kind of understanding that this book gives.

As a citizen of the neighbouring island, I am particularly happy to be associated with a book on the Mass by an Irish priest and scholar. In recent years, at Glenstal, at All Hallows and at Carlow I have had the pleasure of collaborating with Irish priests in the work of the liturgy. It is my belief that England and Ireland have much to offer each other at the deepest levels of the Christian life and it is my hope that such collaboration in this and other fields will be intensified to the mutual benefit of both countries.

J. D. CRICHTON.

1 Opening Rites of Mass

How should Mass begin?

Should Mass begin in a spirit of festive exuberance, with music and "shouts of joy" *(Psalm 46)*, in an atmosphere of mystery and awe, or in a mood of reverential quiet? Should there be a solemn opening with procession, vestments and incense, or an informal one which seeks to keep the liturgy related to daily living?

Uniformity of ritual has passed with the pre-Vatican II era of rubricists. Today, each celebration must be tailored to suit the needs of the particular congregation, the format of celebration and of opening varying as the circumstances of each Mass vary. Mass in a battle-trench will bear little resemblance to Mass in a Carmelite convent. Mass for young children, with all the props of movement, gesture and visual aid which the Church permits[1], will differ from Mass in a crowded city church.

The answer therefore to our initial question is that Mass should begin in the manner which best helps *the particular congregation* to enter into communion with the Creator. For this is the purpose of the Mass, communion. When people assemble for Mass they assemble to *commune* with God. They listen to his Word. They join Christ in praising the Father and in offering sacrifice. The aim of the opening rites is to prepare them, to lift up their hearts, to transform what might well be an unreceptive distracted crowd into an assembly of worshippers, conscious of their identity as the people of God gathered together to celebrate "the memorial of the Lord, the sacrifice of the Eucharist".[2]

Here then is the first duty of the celebrating priest, the first duty of all who are responsible for the "staging" of the celebration: to plan a format of opening which will best dispose the congregation to enter into communion with God.

Opening the Mass means opening men's hearts.

The commentary which follows is basically a commentary on the classic structure of the Mass as contained in the Roman Missal of Paul VI. It envisages a fairly advanced degree of solemnity of the kind suited to the principal Sunday Mass of the average church. For less solemn occasions appropriate modifications can easily be made.

Entrance of celebrant and ministers

The order of procession, as given in the Roman Missal, is:[3]

- a. thurifer,* if incense is used
- b. crossbearer,* flanked by acolytes*
- c. server(s)
- d. reader, who may carry lectionary
- e. celebrant

Route of procession

A direct theatre-like entrance from sacristy to adjacent sanctuary tends to evoke a clericalised era, now happily passed, when the faithful played the role of

* May take part according to circumstances.

"silent spectators" *(Pius XI)*. A procession *through* the assembly seems preferable as it makes for swifter involvement of the faithful, and helps to restore the image of the priest as "a man chosen from among men". For this reason the sacristy[4] should normally be located near the main entrance to the church. If, in an existing church, the sacristy is located near the sanctuary, a procession through the assembly is possible if the priest vests at a table conveniently located near the main entrance.

Incense[5]

Does incense serve any purpose today? One could argue as follows in its favour.

The use of incense is part of our Judaeo-Christian heritage. In Judaism it was a symbol of prayer, of contact with Yahweh: "Let my prayer come before you like incense" *(Psalm 141:2)*. From Judaism—and we must not forget that Christian worship has its roots in Judaism—the use of incense passed into the Christian liturgies of the East and, eventually, the West.[6] The use of incense, therefore, not only links us with our Christian past, but associates us ecumenically with both Judaism and the Orthodox Churches.

The Sunday celebration must speak of values which this world cannot offer. To that celebration the Christian turns in search of something which transcends the ennui of daily living. The celebration must lift him up above the level of the prosaic into the realm of the sacred. This it does through signs, "visible signs signifying invisible things" *(SC 33)*. Incense is such a sign, a symbol of our offering and prayer, a mark of reverence. It helps to create that sense of mystery which is sometimes absent from our renewed liturgy.

It is worth mentioning as a postscript that liturgical

signs should be intelligible *(EM 4)*: the ascending white puffs of incense should be seen but, on the other hand, there is no need for the tintinnabulary one so often hears. In other words, incensation should be seen, not heard.

Processional cross

The carrying of the processional cross can be a telling reminder of the coming of Christ into the assembly. The cross may be placed in the sanctuary, in a receiver in the floor, for example, to serve as a sanctuary cross. Such was the practice in the twelfth century, when the subdeacon, on the arrival of the procession, placed the cross facing the altar.[7] In this practice the present sanctuary cross had its origin.

Early Christian art did not portray Christ on the cross.[8] The artists of the fifth and sixth centuries decked their figureless crosses with flowers and foliage, which sometimes sprouted from the foot of the cross itself. Often they adorned the cross with precious stones. When eventually the figure of Christ appears on the cross it is vested. Many of the Celtic crosses have the vested Christ, e.g. the crosses at Moone, Roscrea, and Cashel. The representation of the sufferings of Christ on the cross, in isolation from his triumph, is the heritage of an era when devotion to the glorious Christ had waned.

Today's artist can learn from the restraint shown by his forbears of early Christian times. These, in turn, were influenced by the discretion of the evangelists who narrated the passion.[9] The cross should speak of Christ's triumph as well as of his death.[10] The Christ who died has risen. This is the message of the glorious cross. Christ is risen! Christ will come again!

Servers

Serving at the altar is a true liturgical ministry. The missal describes servers as *ministers (IG 68)*. They have the right to receive from the chalice *(de iudicio episcopi,* etc. *IG 242).*

Although the presence in the sanctuary of the "flower-pot" type of altarserver, without a function to perform, scarcely seems desirable, the priest should hesitate before excluding such a boy from the sanctuary. Rather should he provide him with some specific task. Pope Paul VI has pointed out that serving at the altar is "a sublime school" for the deepening of the altarboy's understanding of the Eucharist.[11]

The reader

The lay reader "has his own proper function in the celebration, and should exercise that function even when ministers of a higher rank are present" *(IG 66)*. His reading should be "so clear that the faithful will be able to hear it easily and grasp its meaning" *(EM 20)*.

Lay readers, no less than priests, come in for their share of criticism. An unprepared reader may succeed in communicating only his own carelessness.[12] Readers should rehearse in the church itself. An opportune time for rehearsing is on Saturday night when the church is empty after confessions.

The following guidance for lectors and priests was given by the United States Bishops' Commission on the Liturgical Apostolate in a statement issued 29 October 1964:

All scripture readings are to be proclamations, not mere recitations. Lectors and priests should approach the public reading of the Bible with full awareness that it is their honoured task to render the official proclamation of the revealed word of God to his assembled holy people. The character of this reading is such that it must convey that special reverence which is due the sacred scripture above all other words.

(1) It is of fundamental importance that the reader communicate the fullest meaning of the passage. Without exaggerated emphasis or affectation he must convey the particular significance of those words, phrases, clauses or sentences which constitute the point being made. Careful phrasing and inflection are necessary to enable the listener to follow every thought and the relationships among them. Patterns of speech, especially monotonous patterns of speech, must be avoided, and the pattern of thought in the text must be adhered to. The message in all its meaning must be earnestly communicated.

(2) The manner of speaking and tone of voice should be clear and firm, never indifferent or uncertain. The reader should not draw attention to himself either by being nervous and awkward or by being obviously conscious of a talent for dramatic reading. It is the message that should be remembered not the one who reads it. The voice should be reverent without being unctuous, loud without shouting, authoritative without being offensive or overbearing. The pace must be geared to understanding—never hurried, never dragged.

(3) By his voice, attitude and physical bearing, the reader should convey the dignity and sacredness of the occasion. His role is that of a herald of the

word of God, his function to provide a meaningful encounter with that living word. Perfection in this mission may not always be achieved but it must always and seriously be sought.

In addition to the technical preparation of the reader—his speech training, etc., there is the spiritual preparation. It is imperative that he appreciate the sacredness of the office he is carrying out. Through the words he pronounces, "Christ himself speaks" to the faithful *(SC 7)*. The reader at this moment ceases to be a mere "reader". He becomes a "prophet".[13]

Reverencing the altar[14]

"On reaching the sanctuary the priest reverences[15] the altar by kissing it . . . He may also incense it" *(IG 27)*.

What is an altar? It is a table. Not an ordinary table, but a table set apart, a sacred table. It is around this table that the faithful gather for the Supper of the Lord, during which the sacrifice of the cross, together with the whole paschal event, becomes present. The altar, therefore, should be the focal point of the church. It should be the work of an artist and constructed of worthy materials, its shape and dimensions in keeping with the design of the church. Since the priest is no longer required to move from "epistle side" to "gospel side" the trend nowadays is towards the shorter type altar of earlier centuries.

The altar is the table of the Lord. It is not a sacrificial block. To speak of it as a "sacrificial block" suggests an attitude of exaggerated realism towards the Real Presence. Christ dies now no more. The presence of his sacrifice at Mass is a sacramental presence, as it was at the Last Supper.

The new Missal describes the altar as "the place where the sacrifice of Christ is made present under sacramental signs. It is also the table of the Lord at which the people of God are called to share, during Mass. It is therefore the centre of the act of thanksgiving which is accomplished in the Eucharist" *(IG 259)*.

Entrance song

Ideally the celebration of the Eucharist should open with song. A well-performed entrance song can help knit together the most varied congregation into a worshipping community[16] and create a festive climate appropriate to the Eucharist.

The entrance song can be taken from the Roman Gradual or from the Simple Gradual *(IG 26)*. Because these Gradual chants are scriptural they are particularly suited to the opening of the eucharistic celebration. For it is God who, through his word, calls together the faithful at Mass. The early Christians appreciated this, and spoke of the assembled faithful as the "ecclesia"[17] (from the Greek *kaleo,* "to call"; cf. "église", "eaglais"). Because the faithful are called together by God's word, it is fitting that they hear that word proclaimed in the very act of assembling.

Alternatively, any appropriate hymn may serve as an entrance song *(IG 26)*. In selecting the hymn, one must keep in mind its purpose, which is (a) to open the celebration; (b) to unify the people present; (c) to introduce the particular feast or mystery being celebrated; (d) to accompany the procession *(IG 25)*.

a. To open the celebration: A well-chosen entrance song can help create an atmosphere of worship, focusing the minds of the faithful on the sacred action which is to take place.

b. To unify the assembled people: A well-chosen entrance song can help in transforming those present into a worshipping community. John Chrysostom (d. 407) explains: "Once the singing of the psalm begins, all voices are united into harmonious song. Young and old, rich and poor, men and women, slaves and free— all of us sing the one melody. We form together the one choir. Earth imitates heaven."[18]

c. To introduce the particular feast or mystery: The song should be suited to the particular theme, whether it is the triumph of Easter, the joy of Christmas, the hope of Advent, the peace of the Requiem Mass.

d. To accompany the procession: The song begins with the procession and accompanies it. It does not have to stop abruptly when the celebrant reaches the chair. Rather should it continue until it has fairly achieved its purpose, which is to help prepare the people.[19] Who would shout "that's enough" in the middle of a Hail Mary? Yet like the Hail Mary, hymns are normally written to be sung in full. The point will never be appreciated until we are convinced that to sing in worship is to pray; or, as the Roman Missal states, quoting an ancient proverb: "He prays twice who sings well" *(IG 19).* An "Amen" sung is more expressive than an "Amen" said.

If there is no entrance song, the entrance antiphon is recited. Either the people or a reader recites it, during the celebrant's entrance. Failing its recitation by either people or a reader the celebrant himself recites it, when he has greeted the people.

Before leaving the entrance song it will not be out of place to remind organists and church musicians of what Pope Paul VI had to say at the Tenth International Convention of Church Choirs, 6 April 1970. Calling on them to use their talents as a means of glorifying God and of professing their faith, the Pope said:

"The Pope loves you because you are an outward expression of that Easter joy which ought to permeate all the rites of the liturgical year. You radiate joy. You radiate prayer. You radiate goodness . . . Do not shut yourselves off in narcissistic contemplation of your artistic capabilities. Learn how to guide the congregation. Enliven its song, educate its taste, arouse it to active participation. Add solemnity to the sacred celebrations and infuse joy into them."

The greeting

After the entrance song, priest and people together make the sign of the cross. To achieve uniformity of gesture in the congregation, the celebrant should pause slightly, once his hand touches his forehead, before he begins: "In the name of the Father . . ."

The greeting follows, in one of the three forms given in the missal. Daily repetition of these greetings can tend to reduce them to meaningless lip-prayers, unless the celebrant keeps in mind their profound scriptural and theological content.

a. "The Lord be with you".[20]

This is one of the most ancient prayers of the liturgy, rooted in scripture, and rich in its theological content.

Already it appears in the pages of the Old Testament. Boaz, for example, when he arrives at the cornfield in Bethlehem, greets Ruth and the reapers with the words: "The Lord be with you"—to which they reply: "The Lord bless you." A comparison of the different contexts in which the expression is used shows that the Lord's presence with the Israelites connoted primarily his presence as protector and helper. Cf. *Jeremiah 30:10*— "I am with you, says the Lord, to deliver you." Or

Genesis 26:24—"I am the God of your father Abraham. Fear not, for I am with you. I will bless you."

In the New Testament, God's presence among his people finds its full realisation in the person of Jesus, Emmanuel—God with us. Paul adverts to this when he takes over the Old Testament phrase to greet the readers of his epistles: "May the Lord be with you" is his greeting to the Thessalonians *(2 Thess 3:16)*. Here the term "Lord" has a new connotation. It refers to the Lord Jesus, Jesus glorified, Jesus established by the resurrection as Lord and ruler of the universe. Christian use of the phrase "The Lord be with you" is linked also with the Christian's awareness of the presence of the glorified Jesus in the Church, a presence which has been assured for "all days, even to the consummation of the world".

At an early date our greeting passed into the liturgy. We find it, for example, in the earliest extant text of Mass, which is that of Hippolytus, c. 200 A.D., where it occurs exactly as today in the dialogue before the Preface.

One can sum up in the light of the scriptural and liturgical background the meaning of "The Lord be with you" as follows: it is a reminder to the assembled faithful that the eternal inaccessible God has descended into time, and that he is there in their midst in the person of the glorified Lord Jesus: "Where two or three are gathered together in my name, there am I in the midst of them" *(Mt 18:20)*. It is at the same time a prayer that the faithful may benefit to the full, and continue to benefit to the full, from the guidance and protection of the Lord's presence. And since the celebrant too stands in need of this guidance and protection, the faithful reciprocate the prayer with their response: "And also with you".

b. "The grace of our Lord Jesus Christ and the

love of God and the fellowship of the Holy Spirit be with you all."

c. "The grace and peace of God our Father and the Lord Jesus Christ be with you."

These two greetings are to be found at the end of some of the Pauline epistles *(2 Cor 13:14;* cf. *Eph 6:23, 24).* It is probable that they were used at the beginning of Mass in Paul's day. Paul inserted them knowing that the Eucharist would follow immediately the reading of his letter in the assembled community.[21]

"Grace . . . be with you." "Grace" means "favour", the favour or merciful kindness of God. The greeting is a prayer that those assembled will always enjoy God's favour. "The grace of our Lord Jesus Christ"—God's favour comes through the mediation of our Lord.

". . . the love of God . . . be with you." The phrase recalls the love the Father has for us *(Rom 5:8; John 3:16,* etc.). Here it is a prayer that the Father will stir up a response of love within us.

". . . the fellowship of the Holy Spirit be with you." This is a prayer that the faithful will maintain and deepen their union with the Spirit, and with one another.

". . . peace . . . be with you." "Peace" was the ordinary greeting of the ancient Easterns.[22] It was Christ's greeting to the disciples after his resurrection. In Christian writings it came to be the supreme objective of the divine plan. McKenzie describes it as "good order, harmony, communion with God . . . a state of interior calm and of harmonious relations with the Christian community."[23]

The celebrant should *look* at the people as he greets them, allowing his gaze to move around so that all will feel included. The late Father Gerard Kinsella demonstrated, through video-tape experiments at Carlow College, how incredibly strange the celebrant can appear if he greets the congregation with head twisted sideways, while reading from a book or chart. Even the most forgetful among us should scarcely find it overtaxing to dispense with book and chart for such simple interventions as the opening greeting.

Introducing the Mass

The new rite of Mass can put heavy demands on the celebrant, especially if he learned to celebrate under the old régime of the Pius V missal. The mere carrying out of the rubrics is not enough.[24] Every word, every gesture must be meaningful. Of particular importance are those moments at Mass when the celebrant may intervene with a few words of comment or explanation. These moments include:[25]

the beginning of Mass, following the greeting,
before the collect, to remind the people of God's presence, and to invite them to pray for their own particular needs,
before the readings, collectively or one by one,
before the introductory dialogue to the Preface, to mention special motives for thanksgiving,
before the Our Father,
at the "This is the Lamb of God . . ." as an alternative or elaboration after Communion, to lead the people in prayers of praise, without undue takeover of the silence,
at the end of Mass before the final greeting and blessing.

Here we are concerned with the few words at the beginning of Mass. The aim is to help prepare the people, to knit them together into a worshipping community. The words used must be carefully prepared and succinctly worded (IG 68a). They should be human, personal. Reference could be made, for example, to the particular feast or mystery being celebrated, or to the particular congregation or occasion (e.g. marriage, funeral). Well prepared comments create atmosphere, give tone to the celebration, and establish a rapport between the celebrant and faithful which can last throughout the entire celebration.

On the other hand, verbosity can be worse than omission. One thinks, in this connection, of priests who, with an over-concern to give instant meaning to every word and gesture, meander and digress to a painful degree at every turn of the celebration. "Very few words" are to be used, the missal wisely counsels, at these moments of intervention.

Penitential rite

"Before prayer prepare thy soul . . ." Before entering into communion with the divinity, we hesitate. We feel the need for purification, for reconciliation with God and with men. "First be reconciled . . ." our Lord tells us *(Mt 5:24)*. This idea of reconciliation before the celebration of the Eucharist was uppermost in the mind of the author of the *Didaché* (100 A.D.), when he wrote: "Gather together on the day of the Lord. Break bread and give thanks . . . He who has had a difference with a companion ought not to join you until he is first reconciled lest he profane your sacrifice." Paul too calls for this self-examination before the Eucharist: "Everyone should examine himself and with this attitude eat the bread and drink from the cup" *(1 Cor 11:28)*.

Hence the pause for reflection and prayer which the celebrant introduces with the words: "My brothers and sisters, to prepare ourselves to celebrate the sacred mysteries, let us call to mind our sins."

"Let us call to mind our sins" is not the happiest

translation of the missal's "agnoscamus peccata nostra". Some cynics see it as an invitation to delectatio morosa! Alternative words may be used.[26]

In addition to the "Confiteor" the missal gives two other forms of penitential rite. Celebrants should avail of the choice: otherwise the celebration could become tedious. The Congregation of Rites recommends that "the format of celebration should be varied as much as possible".[27] Archbishop Bugnini, secretary of the Congregation of Divine Worship, says: "Where there are several arrangements of a text we should not confine ourselves to a wearisome repetition of the first one. All should be availed of. There is a freshness in variety."[28]

Moreover, in the third form of the penitential rite the celebrant may substitute his own phrases for those given in the missal. In preparing them, he might well draw inspiration from the readings of the Mass. An example for use at a funeral Mass illustrates the point:

"Lord, on this day you console us with the assurance that our homeland is in heaven (first reading). For our failure to remember this amid the anxieties of daily living we ask your forgiveness: Lord, have mercy . . .

"If I should walk in the valley of darkness no evil will I fear *(Resp. Psalm)*. For our lack of hope in times of despair, Lord, we ask your forgiveness: Christ, have mercy . . .

"I am the resurrection and the life. Whoever believes in me shall never die (third reading). Lord, for our lack of faith in your promise, and for all our sins, we ask your forgiveness. Lord, have mercy . . ."

Kyrie eleison

This was an invocation, like our now rather worn out "Lord, hear us" in the "prayers of the faithful" of the early centuries. In 598, the Pope, St Gregory the Great, in an effort to shorten the liturgical celebration, removed the "prayers of the faithful" from the Mass, retaining only the "Kyrie eleison" invocation—an arrangement which lasted, unhappily, down to Vatican II. The new Missal restored the prayers of the faithful before the preparation of the gifts, but retained the "Kyrie" as part of the penitential rite.

Today the "Kyrie" follows the "Confiteor", if the first form of the penitential rite is used.

In singing the invocation it is well on occasion to use the ancient Greek "Kyrie eleison! Christe eleison!" The words are a link with our past, as well as with the Eastern rite Churches. Some people may object, on the grounds that they do not understand Greek. But the words are no less meaningful than words like "Amen" or "Alleluia". The expressions are easily explained. Moreover, how often we find that people who object to the little "Kyrie" on the grounds that it is in an unknown language do not hesitate to use a word like "Kumbaya" in their hymn singing.[29]

Gloria

The "Gloria" is one of the rare specimens of that early Christian hymnody to which Paul alludes in *Col 3:16*. "Sing psalms and hymns and spiritual songs with thankfulness in your hearts to God . . ." Originally the "Gloria" was not a Mass hymn, but a song from morning service. Eventually it crept into the Mass via the Christmas liturgy, because of the words of the angels' song at Bethlehem, with which it begins. By the eleventh century it was in general use in festival Masses.

The "Gloria" has been variously described as "a liturgical pearl",[30] "the most beautiful, the most popular and the most ancient of Christian hymns",[31] "a symphony of acclamations and supplications".[32]

Collect

A short pause should follow the "Let us pray", to allow people remind themselves that they are in the presence of God, and to formulate mentally their private petitions.

Unfortunately, too many celebrants omit this silent pause, and having invited the people to pray, stifle their efforts by proceeding immediately with the "Collect".

In the "Collect" the priest "collects" the people's petitions and presents them to the Father through the mediatorship of the Son, in the Holy Spirit, thus exercising his role of presiding over the assembly in the place of Christ (IG 10).

Romano Guardini says,[33] about this conclusion to the Collect, that it contains the whole law of liturgical prayer. In it he distinguishes the goal, the way, and the power. The goal is the Father, whose face we are seeking. The way is Christ. The power is the Spirit. In the strength of the Spirit we return to the Father along the road of Christ.

The conclusion should therefore be prayed with care, such care as will evoke from the faithful a firm and sincere response, "Amen!"

2 Liturgy of the Word

Before the Council the Word of God was given short shrift at Mass. Only a limited selection of Scripture was read—in Latin. In many churches neither vernacular translation nor homily were given with the result that the faithful often went hungry from the table of God's word. In the catechisms the Word was not considered a principal part of the Mass; offertory, consecration and priest's communion were in a higher category.

Vatican II changed all that. "Richer fare is to be offered to the faithful at the table of God's Word . . . The treasures of the Bible are to be opened up more lavishly . . . A more representative part of the scriptures is to be read to the people . . . The homily is to be highly esteemed as part of the liturgy . . . It is not to be omitted on Sundays and holidays . . .".[1]

It is not difficult to discern the work of the Spirit in this move on the part of the Fathers of Vatican II.[2] Five years after the Council came the new lectionary. The result is that once more after a lapse of centuries the richest passages of sacred scripture are being heard in church. Never since the early years of Christianity has such an effort been made to ensure that the faithful are nourished adequately at the table of God's Word. At least in theory . . .

In practice, the Word is not taking root in the hearts of the faithful, in many instances, at Mass. Why? Because it is not heard? Because the reader is inaudible? Because the scripture passages are difficult? Too often it is because the celebrant himself has not grasped the meaning and spirit of the celebration of the Word. He has not discovered Christ's presence in the Word. He fails to see the relevance of certain Old Testament readings. He looks on the Word as mere instruction.

If the liturgy of the Word is to be celebrated effectively, the following principles must be kept in mind:

1. *When the Scriptures are read in the Church, it is Christ himself who speaks to us.*

This is a direct quotation from the *Liturgy Constitution*.[3] *Christ himself speaks to us* . . . This presence of Christ in the Word is a *real* presence.[4] Augustine says: "Let us listen to the Gospel as if the Lord were there before us, speaking to us . . ."[5] Small wonder, therefore, that the Church has always honoured the divine scriptures as she honours the body of the Lord *(DV 21)*. During Solemn Mass the gospel-book is carried in procession between two lighted candles and preceded by a thurifer. The priest honours Christ's presence in the scriptures by bowing in prayer before he reads the gospel and by kissing the book when he concludes. The faithful honour it by standing for the gospel and by greeting Christ with "Glory to you, O Lord!" "Praise to you, Lord Jesus Christ!" In the eastern rite liturgy the presence is highlighted even more effectively in the acclamations: "Come, let us adore, let us prostrate ourselves before Christ" *(Byzantine rite)*. "Let us listen with reverence and purity of heart to the living words of our Lord" *(Syrian)*. "Teach us your law, O Lord. Make us attentive to your word" *(Chaldean)*. The fact that our reverence for Christ's presence in the scriptures reaches a climax at the gospel does not mean that Christ is not present too in the readings which precede the gospel. He is present in and he speaks through all the readings. That is why the Fathers used to say that to treat any part of the Word of God with negligence was as blameworthy as to let a particle of the consecrated bread fall to the ground.[6]

2. *Christ speaks to us in the Old Testament readings no less than in the New*

Imagine yourself seated in church at Sunday Mass. The first reading has just begun: ". . . from the book of Exodus. The Amelikites came and attacked Israel at Rephidim. Moses said to Joshua . . ." Beside you a teenage girl is studying her fingernails. In front a mother struggles with two restless children. You try to concentrate. ". . . as long as Moses kept his arms raised, Israel had the advantage . . ." What on earth . . .? What message has this for the anxious parents, the distracted teenagers and the bewildered "elders" who make up the congregation? What relevance has it all—Exodus, Amelik, Reph . . . whatever it is ?

The reading in question is relevant because all scripture is relevant. "All scripture is inspired by God. Whatever was written in former days was written for our instruction" *(Rom 15:4; 2 Tim 3:16)*. This is why the Church has rejected the temptation to omit the Old Testament readings from the new lectionary—because the entire Bible speaks of Christ, the Old Testament as well as the New. The point is graphically illustrated in the Emmaus incident where Christ "beginning with Moses and all the prophets interpreted to them (the disciples) in all the scriptures the things concerning himself" *(Luke 24:27)*; and again in the resurrection scene with the apostles where Christ referred to "everything written about me in the law of Moses and the prophets and the psalms" *(Luke 24:44)*. One can understand why St Jerome used to insist that "ignorance of the scriptures is ignorance of Christ"; the saint wrote this without making any distinction between Old and New Testament. The word of God "endures for ever"

(Is 40:8) and it is addressed to us no less than to the Israelites. This is understandable: it is the eternal, immutable God who speaks. Moreover, the people in the Bible are real people with the same kind of human problems, faults, failings and virtues that we have ourselves. The word is "for our instruction" *(Rom 15:4)* no less than for theirs.

3. *The Word is not merely instruction; it is proclamation.*

True, the Word instructs us as to how we should live and what we should believe. But, much more, it is a "proclamation", a "crying-out" in praise of the *mirabilia Dei,* God's wonderful works carried out by him in the past *and today.* With God there is no past, no future. All is an eternal *today,* the *hodie* of the liturgy. God continues to intervene in human history: "yesterday, today, and the same for ever" *(Heb 13:8).* In the Word, therefore, the veil is lifted back from the face of God, we glimpse some aspect of his greatness, and we *proclaim* him.

Because the Word is a proclamation of God's greatness, and not a mere moment of instruction, it may never be replaced by secular readings. To say this is not to reject the use of secular readings, in addition to the scripture passages, for purposes of illustration and application. Moreover, the liturgy of the Word, since it is proclamation, is not just a preparation for the eucharist; it is a celebration in its own right. Nevertheless, what is "proclaimed" in the Word is actualised in the Eucharist: "The faithful should realise that the wonders proclaimed in the Word of God culminate in the paschal mystery, of which the memorial is sacramentally celebrated in the Eucharist. In this way the faithful will be nourished by the Word . . . and in a spirit of thanksgiving will be led to a fruitful participation in the mysteries of salvation."[7]

The proclamation of the sacred text ought to be solemnised, occasionally, through chant. This is especially desirable if the text is of a particularly lyrical quality, e.g. the famous hymn of *Phil 2:5–11*. "Let that mind be in you which was in Christ Jesus, who being in the form of God . . ."

4. *Not only does the Word invite the faithful to make a response; it gives them the strength to make that response.*

The Word evokes from us a response. We verbalise that response in prayer—in the responsorial psalm, the "Glory to you, O Lord", the "Praise to you, Lord Jesus Christ". But more, we live out our response in our daily lives. Here, we are helped by the sacramental power of the Word. St Thomas calls it an *invitatio attrahens et movens ad credendum*.[8] It is the very power of Christ. "The Word of God is living and active, sharper than any two-edged sword . . . it is the power of God . . . at work in you, believers" *(Heb 4:12; 1 Cor 1:18; 1 Thess 2:13)*. The point finds effective expression in one of the Office of Readings hymns:

> Word of God, come down on earth
> Touch our hearts and bring to birth
> Faith and hope and love unending.

5. *The primary concern of each person listening to the Word should be to ask: what is God saying to me now, today?*

This follows from the preceding points. Christ is present in the Word. Christ is speaking to us. It is for us to open our hearts. "O that *today* you would listen to his voice" *(Psalm 94)*. To help stimulate the congregation's interest in the readings, the celebrant should give a brief introduction to the readings *(IG 11)*. One cannot rely on the receptiveness of the average congregation. A neatly-phrased introduction helps to stimulate active listening. The present lectionary offers an introductory phrase before each reading; but these phrases were never intended as a substitute for the recommended "few words" of introduction. The celebrant would be well advised therefore to prepare his own introduction. This ought not to be a mini-homily but an aptly-worded sentence or two designed to arouse the congregation's attention and to help them listen with profit to the message which Christ is about to speak to them.

6. *The basic pattern of the liturgy of the Word is not the invention of Vatican II. It can be traced back through early Christian times to the morning prayer services of the Jews.*

That pattern is as follows: reading, with homily; response; prayer.

This basic pattern, from the synagogal services of the Jews, re-appears in the earliest description of the Eucharist outside the New Testament, written by Justin in 150 A.D.: "On that day named after the sun, all who live in towns and country should gather together for a communal celebration. Then the memoirs of the apostles or the writings of the prophets are read as long as time permits. When the reader has finished his task the president gives an address, urging his hearers to practise these beautiful teachings. Then all stand up and recite prayers . . ." *(Justin's First Apology).*

7. *The dignity of the Word of God demands that the Church have a suitable place for announcing his message.*

Generally the Word should be proclaimed at a permanent ambo. The ambo is not just functional, a book-stand. By its very design and location it should speak of the reverence due to the Word. It should clearly mark out a special *place* in church where something of the utmost importance takes place.

"The dignity of the Word of God demands that the church have a suitable place for announcing his message so that the attention of the people will be easily directed to that place during the liturgy of the Word. Generally the Word of God should be proclaimed at a permanent ambo and not at a movable stand. The ambo should be placed in such a way that the readers may easily be seen and heard by the faithful. The readings, responsorial psalm and Exsultet are proclaimed from the ambo. It may be used also for the homily and the prayer of the faithful. It is not suitable for the commentator, cantor, or choirmaster to use the ambo. The position, distinctive design, and form of the ambo should express its relationship to the altar and the dignity of the Word of God. Where there is a separate platform for the altar the ambo should not normally be placed on it or on its steps. Neither should the ambo be placed alongside the altar."[9]

The Responsorial Psalm

In the responsorial psalm, the people respond to God's message in words given by God himself, the psalms. The particular psalm verses which are used normally continue the theme of the first reading. Ideally a cantor should sing the responsorial psalm. The people listen, and if possible join—ideally by singing—in the refrain.

The repetitious exclamation "response", "response", with which readers sometimes prompt the people's response seems artificial, and indeed infantile. A change in tempo and pitch can be just as effective and far more dignified. Before beginning the psalm the reader should announce clearly the response for the benefit of the congregation, inviting them to repeat it once.

The Alleluia Verse

The Alleluia or chant before the gospel is primarily a salute to Christ present in the Word. It can be highlighted by a gospel procession in which the lectionary is carried by the priest to the ambo, and held aloft during the singing of the "Alleluia". Experimentation will be needed here. The lectionary could be placed on the altar at the beginning of Mass, and a second small lectionary used by the lay reader. Alternatively, the lay reader could leave the lectionary on the altar after reading from it. A suitable chant should accompany the procession. Candles and thurible may be carried. To heighten the solemnity the book might be held aloft again after the reading of the gospel, and the Alleluia repeated in place of the spoken "Praise to you, Lord Jesus Christ".

The homily

"The key to the renewal of the Church in the world today is *the homily*." This is the opinion of the eminent Dom Bernard Botte, O.S.B., of Mount César, Belgium. The question we tackle here is: what precisely is the homily? It is neither a sermon, nor a ferverino, nor a catechetical instruction. What is it? Why did Vatican II impose it as an obligation at all Sunday and holyday Masses?

The Roman Missal describes the homily as "an integral part of the liturgy, a necessary source of nourishment for the Christian life. It ought to be an explanation of some aspect of the readings, or of another text from the

Ordinary of Proper. The homilist should take account of the mystery being celebrated and the needs of the particular community involved."[10] In the liturgy of the Word, Christ speaks to the people. It is for the homilist to explain and actualise the text, to apply it to the needs of the worshipping community, to let them hear the voice of Christ. The homily is not the moment for moralising on some topic which bears no relationship to the sacred text, no matter how useful this may appear to be ("Today, dear people, I am going to speak on the evil of drunkenness . . ."). Christ himself speaks! It is the task of the homilist to help the people hear what Christ is saying, to absorb his message, to reform their lives in the light of that message and with the strength of the Eucharist. The following is a summary of a memorable talk on the homily given by Father Lucien Deiss at the Carlow Liturgy Seminar of May 1972. In sketching the talk I have borrowed from Father Deiss's treatment of the same subject in *Assemblée Nouvelle,* no. 4:

1. The homily is a celebration of Christ

   The liturgy of the Word is a celebration of Christ. Christ is present in the Word. Really present *(EM9)*. The community worships the same Christ in both the liturgy of the Word and the liturgy of the Eucharist. Through the Word he speaks to the community. The purpose of the homily is to help the community hear his voice . . .

   The homily then is not just a pious preparation for the Eucharist proper. Neither is it mere instruction. The Christian life is not just the knowledge of a set of truths and morals. It is Christ. "For me, to live is Christ" says Paul. Hence the homily may never be replaced by a "catechetical instruction", in the sense of a religion lesson.

Here is the real test of the homily: has it helped the congregation to celebrate Christ, to worship Christ by taking to heart his message? Has it helped the congregation to hear Christ's voice in the readings, to recognise him in the responsorial psalm, to respond to his Word in the prayer of the faithful?

Father Deiss showed how the Church in her approach to the Word, as outlined, has followed the Jewish tradition. In the synagogue, the reading of scripture was never a mere reading; it was always a celebration of God.

2. The homily is the actualisation of the Word for the particular community

The homilist must show the particular worshippers how the Word they have heard is relevant for them, helping them to hear Christ's voice and see Christ's face in the sacred text. He must lead the congregation to look at itself, its joys, its sorrows, its problems, and judge them all in the light of the Word.

Father Deiss analysed the Bible's two outstanding examples of homily—those of Ezra and Jesus.

a. The homily of Ezra *(Nehemiah 8)*
Outline: (1) God assembles his people, after the exile in Babylon. (2) He gives them his Word—Ezra reads to the people the book of the covenant. The people accept the Word. (3) The people celebrate the convenant by eating and drinking

with joy "because they had understood the words
that were declared to them" *(v. 8)*.

This is also the structure of the Mass: (1) God
assembles his people. (2) He gives them his Word.
(3) They accept it, and celebrate the covenant by
"eating and drinking with joy" the Eucharist.

b. The homily of Jesus *(Luke 4:16f.)*
Jesus, in the synagogue, after reading from Isaiah,
"sat down and began to say . . . 'Today this scripture
has been fulfilled in your hearing.' " Here is an
outstanding example of how the homily is the
actualisation of the Word for the benefit of the
worshipping community. Through the Word God
speaks to the community today.

3. Preparation of the homily

In the preparation of the homily there are three
basic stages:
    (1) Find out the strict literal sense of the text.
    (2) Find out its Christological sense—how is
Christ speaking through it.
    (3) Actualise Christ's message, showing how
applies to the faithful today.

4. Some objections

Objection—Certain passages in the lectionary, from
the Old Testament particularly, are not relevant
to our people today?
Answer—The priest who argues thus misunder-
stands the nature of the homily. He has not done his

homework, because this precisely is his function as homilist: to translate, actualise, make relevant that scripture passage for his community; to show the community how Christ, through this passage, speaks to them today—about problems of today. Christ needs the priest's words to speak to the community, just as he needs his hands to break the bread of the Eucharist for them.

Objection—"Secular" readings (i.e. non-scriptural) are sometimes preferable?

Answer—No human being can take the place of Christ. No human word can replace the Word of Christ.

Objection—The homily should be based on theology?

Answer—Theology may serve as a "prelude", but the homily proper begins precisely the moment we understand that today this scripture has been fulfilled for us. To say "God is the Father of Jesus Christ" is theology. To say "God is our Father" is homily.

5. Further points

"It seems to me . . ." One is tempted to reply—on hearing the homilist use such an expression—"We are not concerned with what you think; we want to know what God is saying." We are not entitled to preach our opinions; we are entitled, and bound, to preach the Word of God. Father Deiss admitted to spending three hours each Saturday preparing his homily and committing it to writing. As a young priest he did not do this. He does so now, realising "I am speaking not in my own name, but in the name of God."

Study and prayer. Father Deiss referred humor-
ously to priests "overdeveloped in rugby, under-
developed in scripture". There is need for serious
study of scripture. Need too for prayer. There are
moments when we can only fall to our knees before
the mystery of the Word, asking God to teach us
what to say.

Prepare your homily, Father Deiss concluded. Keep
it brief. Speak not in your own name but in the
name of the Lord. It is through your lips that he
speaks to your people.

The homily at daily Mass

Since the purpose of the homily is to help the
faithful hear the voice of Christ in the scripture readings,
the homily should also be part of daily Mass—even if
only "two or three" *(Mt 18:20)* are present. To say this
is not to be unrealistic. One or two sentences, leading
into a moment of silent reflection on the message, will
suffice. A random example will illustrate the point.
Luke 12:35–40 tells of the men waiting for their master
to return from the wedding feast. The celebrant might
add, following the reading of this gospel: "Jesus tells us
today that he will come at an hour we do not expect.
God grant that we will live always as people who 'stand
ready' (expression from the Gospel) for that hour. Amen."

Father Lucien Deiss presses still further: "Even
when the priest is celebrating Mass alone he should
pause for a few moments to ask in the silence of his
heart: what is God saying to me in his Word today?"[11]

Silence after the homily

At the end of the homily the celebrant may invite
the people to reflect briefly in silence on the message of

the Word. Each member of the congregation should ask himself: what is God saying to me today? The aim of this silence is to allow the Word to penetrate more deeply under the influence of the Spirit, for "there is a threshold in the consciousness of the listener which no one can cross, where the noise of human words dies, and when each one says: Speak, Lord, your servant is listening . . ."[12] The "silences" of the Mass call for sensitive handling by the celebrant; without care they can become empty and tedious. Quiet organ music can facilitate reflection during these moments.

A final point about the homily: the homilist should not make the Sign of the Cross at the end of the homily, according to *Notitiae, 83*. The homily is *part* of the liturgy. The Sign of the Cross tends to put the homily in parenthesis.

The Creed

The new Missal uses the apt expression "Profession of Faith". It sees this profession of faith as the people's assent to the Word which they have heard in the readings and homily *(IG 43)*, and an opportunity for them to recall the teachings of the faith before commencing the eucharistic celebration.

It is desirable that the people know how to sing the Credo in Latin *(IG 19)*. Here the missal has in mind especially the singing of the Credo at international gatherings. Visitors to Rome and Lourdes speak of the vivid impression of the Church's unity which is created by the unison of many voices from many lands singing the great Latin Credo.

Not all commentators favour the inclusion of the Credo at Mass. Some point to the duplication it occasions: "The recital of the mighty acts of God in the eucharistic prayer fulfils the necessary purpose of credal proclamation. . . . The Credo (however) may have value as an act of corporate participation in a summation of the faith . . ."[13] Others find that the Credo tends to interrupt the rhythm of celebration, and maintain that since the prayers of the faithful are to be inspired by the readings and homily they should follow them immediately, without the intervention of the Credo. Others take issue with what has been called the "anti-heretical language" of the Credo (the reference is to certain phrases which were formulated as far back as Nicea in 325 and Constantinople in 381 against certain heresies of the time) and would prefer to see a profession of faith which would be based more directly on scripture and would take account of the errors of our own day. Such a Credo might speak of a Christ whose incarnation brings peace *(Luke 4:14)*, who came to unify the children of God scattered by sin *(John 11:52)* and who was sent to announce good news to the poor *(Luke 4:18)*.

Despite such views as these, the Church has opted for the retention of the Credo in the Mass. It has been part of the Roman liturgy for over 900 years. It is much more than a mere recital of articles of faith. It is a résumé of salvation history, linking the faithful with the early Church's profession of belief in one God, one faith, one baptism. It speaks of the gratitude and the hopes of the baptised community who recite it. They have died with Christ in baptism. In the Credo they look forward to the final glorification with him in "the life of the world to come".

A final question: should the Credo be sung rather than recited at Sunday Mass? Many contend that recitation suits the literary genre of the Credo more than singing. The sung Credo makes for a certain imbalance in the Mass and is better limited to special occasions when the profession of faith is emphasised.

The "Universal Prayer" or prayer of the faithful

One might examine this element of celebration under four heads: (1) involvement of the faithful; (2) variety; (3) scriptural colouring; (4) categories of intention.

(1) Involvement of the faithful. The thrust of the celebration at this point is on the people, as the expression "prayer of the faithful" suggests, rather than on the celebrant. Hence the importance of the involvement of the people. But first, a word on the theological background.

The layman has a duty to pray for mankind. It is part of his priestly function. Through baptism he shares in Christ's priesthood. He is deputed to take his place alongside Christ interceding for mankind before the throne of the Father *(Heb 7:25; 9:24)*. The Mass is his privileged moment of intercession, when he prays "through Christ, with him and in him". There, as the new Missal puts it, the layman is "exercising his priestly function of praying for all mankind" *(IG 45)*.

From the beginning Christians were conscious of this function. Paul kept it before them: "I urge you . . . that intercession be made for all men" *(1 Tim 2:3)*. They put it into practice: "We pray in common for ourselves and for all people in the world" (according to Justin, in his description of the Mass, 150 A.D.). Their insistence that the catechumens leave Mass before the commencement of the "prayer of the faithful" reflected their awareness that only the "faithful", i.e. the baptised, were expressly deputed to exercise this priestly function.

Now, to our question: how to achieve effective involvement of the people? Here I make two suggestions:

a. Have the people announce the "intentions". The celebrant's role is to introduce and conclude the "prayer of the faithful". And only that *(See EM 16)*.

Someone other than he should announce the "intentions" *(IG 45)*.

b. Have the people help in forming the "intentions". With small liturgically advanced groups and religious communities, "intentions" tend to come easily and spontaneously. With the large Sunday congregation there is some difficulty. Furthermore people might be invited to send written notification of their "intentions" (e.g. bereavements, illness, forthcoming marriages, etc.) to the presbytery the previous week. Whatever the solution, some provision should be made for individual lay people who might wish to have a particular intention prayed for.

Finally, where there is more than one priest to a church, joint agreement beforehand about the intentions is important. Otherwise there could be embarrassment in the priest-team. One man for example adverts to a tragedy in the parish and includes it in the "intentions" at his Mass. His confrère does not advert to it and omits it at the next Mass—to the disappointment of the congregation.

(2) Variety. All remember the stereotyped sequence of "intentions" when the "prayer of the faithful" was first restored after Vatican II. Today, in most churches, this has given way to more flexible forms well related to both the readings and to current events. Not so with the people's response "Lord, graciously hear us" which Father Crichton in his excellent *Christian Celebration: The Mass*[14] describes as "a noise so nasty that one wonders how anyone can go on tolerating it"!

Any suitable response (or a pause for silent prayer) may be used, e.g. "Lord, hear our prayer", "Remember us, O Lord", "Kyrie eleison"; or responses appropriate to the particular occasion, e.g. "Come, Lord, and save your people" (Advent), "Jesus, risen from the dead, have mercy on us" (Easter). The celebrant can indicate the response in his introduction, e.g. "Let us now pray for the Church and the world in the words: Lord, hear our prayer". The people repeat: Lord, hear our prayer. At the end of each intention a cue is given, e.g. "For the Pope, that God may guide him, let us pray." The people: "Lord, hear our prayer."

Variety can also be achieved through song. Song, moreover, can add meaning to the people's response, and helps towards better unison. Deiss's *Biblical Hymns and Psalms,* vol. 2,[15] has some attractive settings, especially the "O Lord, hear us we pray, O Lord, give us your love", on p. 91.

(3) "Scriptural colouring." By this we mean that the readings and homily should "colour" or inspire the "intentions". The missal implies this: "Having been nourished by the Word, the people pray for the Church and the world" *(IG 33)*. In the light of the readings and homily, the people see more clearly the needs of the Church and the world, and are led to pray. "The Word . . . turns the Church towards the world and imposes an inescapable intercessory responsibility. . . . The Church thus caught up into intercession bears the world with her as she approaches the Supper."[16] To intercede for the world is not a simple request for divine aid. It is an expression of the community's concern for the world, an expression of commitment to work for the betterment of the world in Christ.

The following are examples of "intentions" based on the word Passiontide: "For all who are crucified with Christ through suffering, that they may see in their sufferings an opportunity of helping in the work of redemption . . ." First Sunday in Lent, Year 2: "For Christians everywhere, that through the sincerity of their lives they may proclaim the good news of Christ (phrase from the Gospel) to the world . . ."

(4) Categories of "intentions". "In the 'universal prayer' or 'Prayer of the faithful' the people pray for all men" *(IG 45)*. As the name implies, the universal prayer is said by all, for all. The faithful at Mass are in communion with the universal Church. They are praying for the entire world *(EM 18)*.

To ensure a certain universal stamp on the "intentions" and to offset the inward-looking tendencies from which some congregations seem to suffer the missal presents a four-point sequence of intentions: (a) for the needs of the Church; (b) for public authorities and the salvation of the world; (c) for the suffering; (d) for the local community *(IG 46)*. This is to be "the normal sequence" and is not therefore a rigid ruling. Within its framework there is room for creativity, for well-prepared intentions which reflect both an appreciation of the scripture message and a sensitiveness to the needs of the day.

The "prayer of the faithful" at daily Mass. The missal recommends the prayer whenever there is a congregation. But, the Master himself assures us, even "two or three" *(Mt 18:20)* are an excellent congregation. Lucien Deiss made this point at the Liturgy Seminar in Carlow in May 1972, adding: "Just as the priest saying Mass alone without even a server should stop for a moment to give himself the homily (asking himself: what is God saying to me in his Word today?) so he should stop too for a moment afterwards to pray for the Church and the world."

We end our discussion of the "prayer of the faithful" with this outline of sequence:

(1) Celebrant's introduction. Its aim: "to catch the people's attention and open their hearts to the Lord".[17] Like the "intentions" it should be coloured by the Word and/or the particular theme of the feast or season.

(2) "Intentions." Announced by member(s) of the congregation. In general, fall into four basic categories. Should be coloured by the Word or liturgical theme. Response should be varied.

(3) Conclusion. Celebrant "collects" people's petitions, presenting them to God.

3   Preparation of the Gifts

Key themes here are:

> gratitude for the gifts of creation;
>
> the community's concern for the underprivileged;
>
> determination to make our entire lives a "living sacrifice";
>
> an awareness of the priestly role of the baptised at Mass.

A changed terminology

"Bread and a cup containing wine mingled with water are brought to the one presiding . . ." (Justin in his *Apologia*).

These words, penned away back in 150 A.D., underline the basic meaning of the "offertory": the placing, on the altar, of the gifts to be consecrated. The corresponding action in the first Mass is described in the simple statement: "Jesus took bread . . . and the cup."

First point of note in the new Missal is the change in terminology. "Preparation of the gifts" replaces the former term "Offertory" which, if taken in the strict sense, was misleading. The change is significant, as

Archbishop Bugnini points out.[1] A couple of decades ago it was commonplace to hear preachers speak of the offertory as the moment of "self-offering" when we should place ourselves, spiritually, on the paten and in the chalice. Theologians of the period debated the significance of the offertory. Was it an offering in the strict, i.e., sacrificial sense? An offering of bread and wine? Distinct from the offering of Christ's body and blood? Or was it a mere symbolic anticipation of Christ's offering?

The debate has ended. The replacing of the term offering by *preparation of the gifts* indicates the Church's concern to offset any anticipation of the one real offering of sacrifice, which takes place during the eucharistic prayer. It is the offering of Christ, together with his Church, to the Father.

Significance of the preparation of the gifts

Basically, as we have pointed out, this part of the Mass consists in the material preparation or setting apart on the altar of the gifts of bread and wine. The gifts point in three directions: to the Creator's "goodness", of which they are symbols; to the human labour through which wheat and grapes and indeed all creation is transformed for human benefit; and, lastly, to the final destiny of the gifts themselves—their conversion into "bread of life" and "spiritual drink".

The bread

"Jesus took bread . . ." The missal stipulates that the bread should be wheaten-bread and, in the Latin rites, unleavened. It recommends *(expedit)* that it should "genuinely look like food" and "be made in such a way that the priest can break it and distribute the parts to at least some of the faithful" *(IG 283)*.

"Unleavened bread . . ." The first generations of Christians used ordinary bread. Gradually the Christians of the West reverted to the use of the unleavened, i.e. unraised, bread of Judaism. Influences behind the change included a concern to make the eucharistic bread distinctive; the association between leaven and corruption *(cf. 1 Cor 5:7 f.)*; and the general tendency of the period to revive certain Old Testament prescriptions.[2] Since the eleventh century, approximately, the use of leavened bread has been prohibited in the Western rites.

"Genuinely looking like food . . ." Here there appears to be an implicit discouragement of the conventional small, white, plastic-type hosts to which we are accustomed. The use of such hosts seems to be at variance with the whole spirit of the renewed liturgy and the Church's concern to "make more intelligible the signs by which the Eucharist is celebrated" *(EM 4)*. Something more substantial, more bread-like, is required.

"Made in such a way that the priest can break it and distribute the parts to at least some of the faithful . . ." The ideal is the single loaf, which may be unpractical for the parish Mass, but is quite manageable for the small group celebration in communities, classrooms, etc. St Paul reflects the appreciation which the early Christians had of the symbolism of the single loaf: "We, though many, form a single body because we all share in this one loaf" *(1 Cor 10:17)*. A first-century prayer says:

> As this bread which we break
> was once scattered on the hills
> and has now been gathered together into one,

so, Lord, gather together your Church
from the ends of the earth
into your kingdom.[3]

The new Missal presses for this gesture of the
"breaking of the bread" on the grounds that "it shows
the Eucharist more clearly as a sign of unity and
charity, since the one bread is divided between the one
family" *(IG 283)*. The description of the Mass as the
"breaking of the bread" is one of the oldest, going back
to the pages of the New Testament *(Luke 24:30;
Acts 2:42, 46;* etc.).

Wine

Luke indicates that Jesus used grape wine *(22:18)*.
Accordingly the missal prescribes "natural wine from
the fruit of the vine, pure and unmixed with any
foreign substance" *(IG 284)*.

Wine has its own symbolism. It stands for joy; to
share wine is to share the joy of others *(Ps 103:15)*.
Canticles 5:1 associates wine with love. Wine too—red
wine—suggests the blood of sacrifice.[4] The single cup of
wine, like the single loaf, symbolises unity. Hence the
importance of avoiding the kind of clutter of chalices and
patens one sometimes sees at concelebrated Masses. The
ideal is: one loaf, one cup.

Preparation of the altar

Not until the commencement of the Preparation of
the Gifts should the corporal, purificator, chalice and
missal be placed upon the altar *(IG 49)*. An elaboration
of this directive would be to wait until this moment also
before putting on the altar the altar-cloth (only one is

now required) and candlesticks. The gesture helps to mark clearly the commencement of the central part of the Mass, the liturgy of the Eucharist.

Sacred vessels

There is greater liberty now in respect of the material and form of chalices, ciboria, etc.[5] One notes especially a trend towards a new dish-style ciborium, large enough to hold the more substantial type of bread (see above) for both the celebrant and communicants.

The procession

Our revived "offertory procession" grew out of the ancient custom by which the faithful brought their own bread, wine and gifts to the church. History records Cyprian's rebuke to the well-to-do lady who used come to church empty-handed, and communicate from bread supplied by the poor: "You ought to blush for shame" he told her.[6] Gifts included, in addition to bread and wine, oil, cheese, fruit, vegetables, flowers, fowl, etc.[7]

Here, once again, history can be our great teacher. Our Christian concern for the underprivileged should somehow find expression in a practical way at the eucharistic celebration. *Acts 2:44* records the generosity of the first eucharistic assemblies who "distributed their goods to all, as any had need". The new Missal expressly mentions the possibility of collecting "gifts for the poor" *(IG 49)* at this moment of Mass.

One method, and it repays experiment, is to place a large hamper at the offertory table, on occasions such as Christmas, world hunger days, etc., for the purpose of receiving the people's gifts of food, clothing, etc. The hamper could be carried in the offertory procession and placed near the altar. After Mass the gifts are taken away for distribution. This suggestion ought not to be taken as encouragement for the indiscriminate inclusion of objects like football boots, hammers, books, etc., in the offertory procession, as symbols of our work and recreation. We grant that such a practice may have a certain pedagogical value, and could be useful in a paraliturgical service, outside Mass. But the Mass is not the place for it. In any case the "objects" mentioned are not gifts, since they are restored to their owners after Mass! Fortunately, such liturgical frippery seems to be on the wane.

But to return to the origins of the offertory procession. It developed in two forms. In the East, the faithful brought their gifts to the sacristy before Mass. At the offertory the ministers carried the gifts from sacristy to altar in solemn procession to the accompaniment of chants like the moving *Cherubikon*, which is sung to this day by the Byzantines. In the West, on the other hand, the procession developed differently. The faithful proceeded to the sanctuary at the offertory, each presenting his gift to the deacon. The rite of the offertory procession continued unbroken in the Eastern liturgies but began to die out in the West during the period of religious decadence in the Dark Ages, leaving as its only trace the "passing of the plate", until its revival after Vatican II.

Traditionally, the offertory procession was linked with the priesthood of the laity. Only the baptised were allowed to take part in it. The carrying of the gifts was seen as an expression of their share, through Baptism, in Christ's priesthood. Hence the missal's reference to the procession as "a fitting expression of the faithful's participation" in the Eucharist *(IG 101)*.

Today the Church recommends the offertory

procession. "It is desirable that the faithful present the
bread and wine" *(IG 49)*. Unfortunately, the revived
procession, in too many instances, has given way to
what must appear to the faithful as a rather purposeless
trimming to the Mass. Those taking part should be
gently coached so that their very bearing and movement
will reflect the reverence due to the gifts destined for
consecration. Solemnity can be heightened by having
two acolytes lead the procession. Gifts are carried: the
bread, the wine, the water—not empty chalices, vessels,
etc.

The money collection

This evolved, as I have already indicated, from the
ancient practice by which the faithful brought gifts from
their homes to the church. Its significance should be kept
before the people. The jingling distractions, about which
so many complain, can be overcome if the celebrant
pauses, sitting down until the collection is over and the
procession with the gifts is ready to begin. Nor will this
cause any appreciable delay, if the collectors are
efficiently organised. During the collection a discreet
organ interlude can be effective.

The offertory song

"The procession . . . is accompanied by the offertory
song which continues at least until the gifts have been
placed upon the altar" *(IG 50)*. The song need not speak
of bread or wine, or of offering. Its purpose is to accompany and arouse communal interest in the procession.

Any appropriate song of praise, rejoicing, thanks, etc., in keeping with the season, may be used. Song is not always necessary, or even desirable, during the preparation of the gifts. Many, in fact, welcome a little "breathing-space" at this point. The liturgy of the Word demands concentration. The liturgy of the Eucharist also calls for eager concentration. A few moments of quiet in between, when the faithful relax in silent meditation, can be a welcome break. "A liturgy is not well constructed", writes Lucien Deiss, "if it demands constant concentration and thus creates constant tension. Prayer is to be a relaxing experience for the soul, not an exasperating one."[8] For this reason it would be well to replace the offertory song, from time to time, with organ or instrumental music; or, alternatively, with a period of silence.[9]

If the offertory song continues after the procession has ended, the celebrant should neither "break in" with the blessing prayers ("Blessed are you, Lord, God . . .") nor wait tediously until the singing stops, but continue immediately, saying the prayers *secreto*.

The prayers

"Blessed are you, Lord, God of all creation . . ." The two blessing-prayers, over the bread and over the wine, have been inspired by the ancient berakoth table-prayers which are said to this day in the homes of pious Jews, and which our Lord himself would have used each time he "blessed" bread at the commencement of a meal: "Blessed are you, Lord our God, king of the world, who cause bread to come forth from the earth; (over the wine: '. . . who give us this fruit of the vine')." In our gratitude we "bless" God, in the biblical praise/thanks sense of the word, for all the gifts of creation, which are represented by the bread and the wine. Our gratitude here is but a prelude—and an acceptable one, we believe, pace the commentators who complain of "duplication"—to the expression of gratitude par excellence which comes with the Eucharistic Prayer.

Note that the celebrant is not obliged to say the prayers aloud; the missal says: "If there is no offertory song, the priest *may* say these words aloud" (19).

"By the mystery of this water and wine . . ." The practice of diluting wine with water was customary in Jesus' time not alone among the Jews but among orientals generally. The reason was a practical one: the wine tended to be of a viscous quality. Dilution was also a certain safeguard against intemperance.

Justin refers to the practice, in the famous *Apologia* passage mentioned earlier: "Bread and a cup containing wine mingled with water are brought to the one presiding." Cyprian, in the third century, gives a symbolic explanation: the mingling of water with the wine represents the union of the people with Christ.[10] Later the mingling came to represent the union of the two natures in Christ. (Hence the resistance to the practice, in the monophysite Armenian rite.)

The accompanying prayer evokes both the incarnation of Christ and the divinisation of the Christian. The prayer is to be said *secreto* (20).

"Lord, God, we ask you to receive us . . ." The prayer is inspired by the prayer of Azariah in *Daniel 3:39–40*. The reference to the "humble and contrite hearts" is a reminder of the integrity of life which should accompany our eucharistic offering. It is in keeping with Paul's exhortation: "I appeal to you, brethren, by the mercies of God, to present your bodies as a living sacrifice, holy and acceptable to God, which is your spiritual worship" *(Rom 12:1)*. Again, this prayer is said *secreto* (22).

Incensation

"The gifts on the altar and the altar itself may be incensed. The incensation signifies the ascent of the Church's offering and prayer to God" *(IG 51)*. There is scarcely any advantage in incensing the altar at this stage if it has already been incensed at the beginning of Mass. The celebrant may choose to incense the gifts alone, or the gifts and people alone. The accompanying prayers of the former rite are no longer of obligation.

The washing of the hands

The gesture of washing the hands, which from its origin seems to have been included for symbolic and not utilitarian (as was commonly believed) reasons, is first mentioned by Cyril of Jerusalem in 348 A.D.[11] The priest washes "his hands" *(IG 52)*—not his thumbs and index fingers only. Here again we see concern for meaningfulness of gesture *(EM 4)*. Likewise the vessels used should be meaningful, worthy and suited to their purpose *(IG 311)*. A dish, a jug, a towel—these would seem to harmonise better with the spirit of the reformed rites than the conventional miniature substitutes.

The accompanying prayer, "Lord, wash away my iniquity . . ." is from the *Miserere (Psalm 50:4)*. It is said *secreto (IG 24)*.

"Pray, brethren . . ."

The first words of the response, "May the Lord accept the sacrifice at your hands . . ." call to mind the point made in Vatican II's *Decree on Priests,* par. 2, that it is through the hands of the priest that the community offers the Eucharist. The rest of the response suggests the two-way purpose of the eucharistic sacrifice: the glory of God and the sanctification of the Church.

Prayer over the offerings

The new rite has dropped the former term "secret" in favour of the more ancient expression "prayer over the offerings". Basically the prayer is a petition that God will accept the gifts and the Mass will benefit us.

The "prayer over the offerings" concludes the rite of presentation of the gifts. At the same time it looks to the final destiny of the gifts, their conversion into the body and blood of Christ, and sounds the overture for the great Eucharistic Prayer which is about to begin.

4 Liturgy of the Eucharist

We come to the heart of the Mass, the great eucharistic prayer. It begins with the dialogue before the preface and ends with the great doxology:

> Through him, with him, in him, in the unity of the holy Spirit, all glory and honour is yours, Almighty Father, for ever and ever. Amen.

What precisely happens during the eucharistic prayer? We base our answer on the wording of the new Missal: the people unite with Christ in (a) proclaiming the wonderful works of God, and (b) offering sacrifice.[1]

At the last supper Jesus, following the Jewish meal-time practice, spoke a prayer over some bread and a cup of wine. The New Testament writers record this when they say he "made a blessing" *(Matthew* and *Mark)* or "gave thanks" *(Paul* and *Luke)*. This grace-before-meals was, and is, known among the Jews as *berakah*. We translate it "eucharistic prayer" or "anaphora".

Basically the berakah (eucharistic prayer, anaphora) is a prayer of praise and thanksgiving to God for all his *mirabilia,* the wonderful deeds he has worked throughout history on behalf of men. Jesus, in praying the berakah at the last supper, went on to identify the bread and wine with his body and blood about to be given in sacrifice. Then, in communicating the apostles with the "eucharistised"[2] or consecrated elements—now his body and blood — he thereby associated them in a most intimate way in his own redemptive work. Their eating and drinking was a communion in the sacrifice present before them in the person of Jesus.

All this is essential for our understanding of the Mass and communion.

At Mass we "do this"—what Jesus did. Like Jesus, the priest addresses a berakah to the Father in the name of the people. It is a proclamation of our praise and thanksgiving to the Father for all his mirabilia, his wonderful works, which reach their high-point in the gift to us of a Redeemer. But more: the Redeemer becomes present to us. The time and space which separate us from the sacrifice which Jesus offered 2,000 years ago in Palestine is telescoped. His sacrifice is present in our midst, here and now. Jesus, crucified, glorified, is present before us, interceding for us, offering himself to the Father, and offering, with himself, us. Our eating and drinking is, as it was for the apostles, a communion in Christ's sacrifice.

A lengthy discussion of the theology of the Mass is outside the scope of the present work. However, a brief examination of the various elements which go to make up the eucharistic prayer will not be out of place. The Eucharistic prayer is itself a statement of what the Church believes and wishes to say about the eucharist; as such it contains a nutshell theology of the Eucharist. That is why we have more than one eucharistic prayer: no single prayer can give adequate expression to the Church's understanding of the Eucharist. Four prayers provide us with four vantage points from which we can view this "heart and climax" of the Mass.[3]

The basic elements common to the hundred or so eucharistic prayers which have come down to us from the early Church are: the thanksgiving, the epiclesis (a later addition, probably), the words of institution, the anamnesis and the doxology. Here we examine them with reference to the three new eucharistic prayers and, to a lesser extent, the Roman Canon.

Dialogue before the Preface

"The Lord be with you ... Let us lift up our hearts . . . Let us give thanks to the Lord our God." Venerable words, these. They go back at least to the year 200 A.D.[4]

"Let us lift up our hearts. . . ." These words are an invitation to us to lift ourselves up in spirit to the throne of grace *(Heb 4:16)* where Jesus in the heavenly liturgy is eternally offering himself to the Father for us. Our brother Christians of the Eastern rites add: "Let us stand with reverence and awe! Let us give heed and offer the holy sacrifice in peace! Let us lift up our hearts with reverence before the Lord!"[5]

"Let us give thanks." Jesus most likely began his eucharistic prayer at the last supper with these words, according to the custom of the time.

The pre-preface dialogue then is a summons to us to leave behind us the cares of this world and lift up our spirits in contemplation of the great mystery about to be accomplished. Crossing the threshold of the world, we take our stand alongside our Lord to praise, thank and intercede with him before the Father.

The Preface

The word here means much more than "introduction" to the eucharistic prayer.[6] *Prae-fari* means to speak out in the presence of someone. It is a proclamation of praise and thanksgiving to God for his marvellous acts on behalf of men. These various acts are spelled out in their various facets in the rich collection of eighty prefaces in the new Roman Missal.

The celebrant should not only be heard and understood as he proclaims this prayer. He has the duty to make the prayer come alive, to convey the very significance of the prayer by the faith, the joy, the gratitude and the enthusiasm behind his words.

The Sanctus

The hymn of the angels! Heaven and earth unite to proclaim (*pro-clamare* means to cry aloud) the majesty and holiness of the creator. No other song can even pretend to the magnificence of the Sanctus.

The chant itself comes from *Isaiah (6:3)* who hears, in ecstacy, the heavenly seraphim sing: Holy, Holy, Holy Lord Sabbaoth! Doubtless Isaiah is here letting us in on the temple liturgy of his day,[7] so that once again we have here, in the Sanctus, a legacy from our spiritual ancestors, the Jews. Although the Sanctus was sung from earliest times in Christian worship, it did not appear in the Mass until later. First mention of it in the Mass of the West is about 400 A.D.[8]

"Thy glory fills all heaven and earth!" Isaiah has "The earth is filled with his glory." What was for Isaiah a statement of fact becomes for us a proclamation of our praise and wonder.

Hosanna! Originally the word meant "save us". Since then it has become a cry of praise to God.

"Blessed is he who comes . . ." The phrase comes from *Psalm 118:26*. At Mass it is applied, as in the Gospel account of Christ's triumphant entry into Jerusalem, to the Messiah.

Few texts have inspired such magnificent musical

compositions as has the Sanctus. Small wonder that musicians of our day enthuse about it as they do. Lucien Deiss would have it sung at every Mass.[9] He argues that "every musical resource should be made available for the Sanctus—full organ, choir, trumpets, etc. Only then should other parts of the Mass be enriched with music."

Transition from the Sanctus

"Father, you are holy indeed . . . we acknowledge your greatness . . ." This brief re-statement of the praise/ thanks theme from the preface leads us on to the next element which is a prayer of intercession.

First epiclesis

The word, from the Greek, means invocation. The epiclesis prays for the coming of the Spirit on the gifts. If Christ's sacrifice is to be made present, if the bread and wine are to become the body and blood of Christ, God himself must intervene. And so we pray the Father to effect the consecration by the power of the Spirit.

Mention of the holy Spirit makes us all the more grateful for the new eucharistic prayers. The ancient and venerable Roman Canon, cherished though it is, makes no such reference to the Spirit in its corresponding pre-consecratory prayer: Bless and approve our offering . . . —an omission of which Western Catholics became more and more aware as interest in the Eastern anaphoras developed.

Narrative of institution

"Here, by the words and actions of Christ, the last supper is made present, that supper in which Christ the

Lord himself instituted the sacrament of his passion and
resurrection when he gave to the apostles his body and
blood under the species of bread and wine, to eat
and drink, and left them with the command to perpet-
uate that same mystery" *(IG 55d)*.

Little can be added to this concise statement from
the missal, except, perhaps, for two points:

(1) The consecration is not the mere (if we may use
such an adjective) changing of bread and wine into the
body and blood of Christ, not the mere making present
of a static Christ. It is the presence in our midst of the
risen glorified Christ, worshipping the Father in an
eternal timeless act, and drawing us sinners into that
worship as we struggle to offer our own miserable selves
to the Father.

(2) The consecration should not and cannot be
isolated from its context.[10] It is part of that single entire
sequence, that great unit which is the eucharistic prayer.
Such "isolation" of the moment of consecration has led
to unhappy results: the reprehensible Middle Ages
practice of rushing to church, staying just for the
consecration, then rushing to another church and yet
another in an effort to "clock-up" as many consecrations
as were physically possible within the limits of a single
Sunday morning in a mediaeval city; the playing down,
in more recent times, of the other great parts of the Mass,
the liturgy of the Word and the Communion which were
forced to cede ground before the one thing that seemed
to really matter.

In pronouncing the words of consecration the priest
should take special care with his manner of speaking.
The disjointed over-unctuous manner of speaking,
common in the days of the Latin Mass, and used as if it
were through the effort and struggle of the priest himself
that transubstantiation was effected, should be avoided.
At the same time his manner of speaking should reflect

the reverence due to the Lord's own words, as well as the priest's own awareness of the great mystery of faith confronting him.

Proclamation of the mystery of faith

This is the third "intervention" by the people in the eucharistic prayer, the first being the preface dialogue, the second the Sanctus, and the final one the great Amen. By means of these interventions or acclamations, the people express their priestly participation in the Eucharist, ratifying what the priest says and does in their name. The post-consecration intervention "Christ has died . . ." or its alternatives is much more than a pious ejaculation of faith in the real presence; it is a profession of faith and hope in the entire "mystery of faith", i.e. the divine plan for our salvation which climaxes in the passion, resurrection, ascension and final coming in glory of the Lord.

Anamnesis

At the last supper Jesus said: "Do this as a memorial of me." The actual word used by our Lord, *zikkaron*,[11] i.e. memorial, or in Greek: anamnesis, had a precise technical meaning: a recalling and actualising of past events. At Mass, through the words of consecration, the great events of Jesus' life—his passion, resurrection and ascension—are not merely recalled, as the Reformers would have us believe; they are actualised in the here and now. In the anamnesis of the Mass we advert to our Lord's command to celebrate this memorial, and mention specifically our offering of sacrifice: "Father, calling to mind the death your Son endured, his glorious resurrection, . . . we offer you in thanksgiving this holy and living sacrifice" *(Eucharistic Prayer 3)*.

Second epiclesis

This is a beautiful communion prayer coming to us in varying forms according to the particular eucharistic prayer. We pray for unity within the Church; for the coming of the Spirit on the participants; the making of the participants into an everlasting gift to the Father, a living sacrifice of praise; we pray for every grace and blessing. It is a prayer, in brief, that the Eucharist will have its effect on our lives.

The intercessions

Every Eucharist is a celebration of the whole Church. The whole Church offers. The whole Church is offered. Particular participants at a particular Mass are linked mystically with their fellow Christians throughout the world, as well as with their departed brothers and sisters. The point is underlined in the intercessions.

Notice the outward-looking character of the prayers. We pray not only for the actual members of the Church, living and dead, but for all who seek God with a sincere heart . . . all the dead whose faith is known to God alone. Particularly beautiful is the special passage for insertion into the third eucharistic prayer, which lingers meditatively on the beatific vision: "On that day we shall see you, our God, as you are. We shall become like you, and praise you for ever through Christ our Lord, from whom all good things come."

Doxology

"Through him, with him, in him. . . ." Our solemn glorification of the Holy Trinity! We worship the Father *through* Christ, our mediator; *with* Christ, the victim of our offering; *in* Christ, that is, abiding in him, united most intimately to him, especially as a result of sacramental communion.

The accompanying gesture, in which paten and chalice are raised aloft, highlights the beauty and importance of this solemn conclusion to the great eucharistic prayer.

The great Amen

A powerful, glorious and majestic moment of the liturgy. The great Amen is the people's moment par excellence! Through it they ratify everything the priest has said and done. In that tiny word is concentrated and expressed all their adoration of God, all their gratitude, all their sorrow, all their needs. In it too is contained their offering of their daily lives to God, their solemn renewal of their covenant pledge to live as children of him who said: "I will be their God, and they shall be my people." Augustine called it our signature to the Mass: "Amen dicere subscribere est."

Much should be made of the great Amen. It is there in our earliest account of the Mass (Justin, *First Apology* 65, 150 A.D.). At the end of the eucharistic prayer, Justin tells us, "all the laity present shout their assent saying 'Amen'." Jerome tells us how the great Amen used sound like a thunder clap in the ancient basilicas. Merely to speak the word is to do less than justice to its majesty and power. It must be sung. Through song, and the prolongation and repetition which it permits, we are able to express our Amen more beautifully and ponder more at length on its meaning.

A further question

Sometimes one finds a certain imbalance in the Mass as between the liturgy of the Word and the liturgy of the Eucharist. The former tends to be long-drawn out. It is surrounded by much action and, at times, song. The eucharistic prayer, by comparison, seems to pale.

Three suggestions could be kept in mind:

First, we must make far greater use of silence at the "offertory" or preparation of the gifts. By this stage of the Mass the people have already been subjected to quite a torrent of words. They need a time for silence, a time for quiet before setting out on their approach to the summit of celebration, the great eucharistic prayer.

Secondly, song can be most effective in lifting up the eucharistic prayer. Song on the part of the people— ideally at the four moments of intervention: pre-preface dialogue, Sanctus, acclamation after consecration, the great Amen. Song on the part of the priest—ideally at the Preface, the words of institution, and great doxology, which, incidentally, will keep the people from joining in what is strictly a presidential prayer.

The people's song gives unity and more meaningful expression to their intercessions. That of the priest gives, in addition, the added solemnity which so befits these great moments.[12] This applies especially to the words of institution, which are not just a narrative, but a solemn proclamation of the mystery being accomplished. Song is particularly effective in a concelebrated Mass, where words spoken together by different concelebrants so often sound discordant. If concelebrants are saying the words of institution, as is the normal case, the voice of the presiding priest should predominate; the voices of the other priests should be subdued.

Finally, the celebrant should avail, at least on occasion, of the possibility which the missal allows him of giving a brief introduction to the eucharistic prayer. In this introduction he can suggest motives for thanksgiving appropriate to the particular assembly, and remind them of the great action about to take place.[13]

5 Communion

Introduction to the Our Father

"Let us pray with confidence to the Father . . ."
Here again the celebrant should bear in mind that he is
not obliged to keep slavishly to the words of the missal.[1]
In varying them he might well draw inspiration from
the Eastern rites where the purpose of the invitatory
before the Our Father is (a) to express our need for
purification, and (b) to arouse in us a sense of wonder as
we make bold (*audemus dicere* in the former Latin rite) to
call God "Father".

Thus we have in the Syrian rite:

"Make us holy, O God, in body and spirit, so that
with pure heart, resplendent soul and open countenance
we might dare to address you as heavenly Father, you
who are all-powerful, all-holy . . .".

Or again:

"Purify us Lord from both our hidden failings and
our open faults . . . May every thought contrary to your
goodness be far from us! May we always present ourselves before you with stainless heart and faultless
conscience, singing, with that confidence which you
have inspired in us: Our Father . . ." *(Coptic, Chaldean
rites)*.

The Our Father

For sixteen hundred years Christians have been
praying the Our Father at Mass. Although the first real

evidence for the practice dates from about 400 A.D. one gets the impression that it was there even in Cyprian's time (258 A.D.).[2] Oscar Cullmann[3] feels that the Our Father was part of the Eucharist as early as the first century, arguing from the inclusion of a doxology or liturgical acclamation in the *Didaché*, where the prayer appears.

Two of its petitions make the Our Father particularly suitable as a prayer before Communion. First, the petition "Give us this day our daily bread". Biblical scholars continue to discuss the precise meaning of "daily bread". Jeremias understands the term in an eschatalogical sense as the bread of eternal life, which includes everything we need in the here and now for both body and soul.[4] In the context of the eucharist the thrust of the petition is obviously on the eucharistic bread of sacramental communion. This "eucharistic" interpretation of the phrase is common among the Fathers.

The petition "Forgive us our trespasses as we forgive . . ." implies the forgiveness of others, which is a prerequisite for the acceptance by God of our sacrifice. How conscious the first Christians were of the need for mutual love and forgiveness is reflected in the directive of the *Didaché* (c. 100 A.D.) which says: "Let him who has had a difference with his companion not join you (in the Eucharist) before he is first reconciled, lest he profane your sacrifice . . .".

"Deliver us . . ." The old form of this embolism in the Latin rite invoked our Lady, the apostles Peter, Paul, Andrew and all the saints. The revised form, in the new Missal, is abbreviated, but has a beautiful addition from *Titus 2:13* : "as we wait in joyful hope for the coming of our Saviour, Jesus Christ".

"For the kingdom, the power and the glory are yours . . .". This doxology breathes hope and joy. Some manuscripts of the St Matthew gospel give it with the Our Father. The *Didaché* too gives it, in a slightly different form. The Eastern and Protestant liturgies use it.

The rite of peace

"Lord Jesus Christ, you said to your Apostles: I leave you peace . . .". This is a prayer for peace and unity, "the ecumenical prayer par excellence"[5] *(Max Thurian).* "Peace" here is peace in its biblical sense, which is much wider than the ordinary sense of the word. It is the state of a person who lives in harmony with himself, with nature, with the Christian community, with God.[6] "Unity", the building up of the Church in unity, is the real, the ultimate effect of the Eucharist, as St Thomas said seven hundred years ago.[7]

The accompanying gesture, the kiss of peace, has a long history, and is traceable back to Old Testament times. The most famous of the early accounts of the Mass testify to it: Justin (150 A.D.), Hippolytus (c. 200), Augustine (354–430), *Apostolic Constitutions* (4th century?), Cyril of Jerusalem (c. 400 A.D.).

Justin mentions that "after finishing the prayers, i.e. of the faithful, we greet each other with a holy kiss." Augustine writes: "after the Our Father the Christians say 'peace be with you' and kiss one another with a holy kiss."[8]

By the Middle Ages, the only trace of the gesture in the Western rite low Mass was the kiss of peace given by the celebrant to the altar.

The new Missal has restored the rite. Through it "the faithful implore peace and unity for the Church and for all mankind, and express among themselves mutual love before they share the one bread" *(IG 56b).*

The missal adds that the form of the gesture is to be decided by the episcopal conference, in the light of local conditions.

The U.S.A. Bishops' Committee for the Liturgy points out, in a pastoral commentary on this question,[9] that the kiss of peace is not in the order of a greeting, welcome or hello. Nor is it meant to occasion a big handshaking party.[10] It is, rather, a *prayer and sign,* a personal and sincere pledge of reconciliation and peace in view of the communion which is to follow and also in view of what took place before. An appropriate prayer may be added to the greeting, such as "Peace be with you, N." Experience indicates that a gentle, sound and ongoing catechesis softens opposition to the gesture, and gradually leads people to full acceptance of it.

Where the gesture is not practised, then, pending its introduction, a word from the celebrant inviting the faithful to pause and mentally put themselves at peace with one another, forgiving one another, etc. can be most effective.

The fraction and Agnus Dei

The gesture of "breaking of the Bread" carries a powerful meaning, and gave its name to the entire Mass in apostolic times. It is not only a repetition of what Jesus did at the Last Supper, it is symbolic of that unity which should exist among Christians. The breaking of the Bread and the communicating of at least some of the faithful with it, brings out that "we, though many, are one body, because we all share in the one Bread" (*I Cor 10.17*). That is why the priest should (*IG 283*) consecrate a host large enough for the communion of at least some of the faithful as well as for himself.

The purpose of the Agnus Dei chant is to accompany

the fraction. The invocation may be repeated as long as is necessary for this purpose—a point to be remembered especially in concelebrated Masses.

The mingling of the broken portion of the host with the precious Blood refers to the unity of the body and blood of Jesus, who is risen, alive and present.

Private prayer before Communion

Some celebrants, one notices, say aloud the prayer: "Lord Jesus Christ, Son of the living God . . .". The temptation to do this is understandable. It is a beautiful prayer. However, the missal directs that the prayer be said *secreto (114)* adding "the priest prepares himself through silent prayer, so that he may receive Christ's body and blood fruitfully; the faithful do likewise, praying silently" *(56f.)*. These moments of silence relieve the faithful from what Father J. G. McGarry once described to me as "the battering with words" which tends to be a characteristic of our celebrations at present.

"This is the Lamb of God . . ."

Here again the priest might vary the missal words. Recalling the homily message at this point can be effective. For example, if the homily message is on Christian love, the celebrant might say as he holds up the host before the people: "This is Jesus Christ who calls upon us this day to love one another. This is the Lamb of God who takes away the sins of the world . . ."

The addition of the 1970 missal "Happy are those who are called to his Supper" is inspired by *Apoc 19:9*. The faithful respond in an act of humility prompted by the Gospel words: "Lord, I am not worthy . . ."

Reception of Holy Communion

Holy communion is like a multi-faceted jewel. Here we view it from three aspects:

Communion as intimate union with our Lord.

Communion as a sharing in the redemptive work of Christ.

Communion as union with one another.

1. Communion, intimate union with our Lord

" He that eats my flesh and drinks my blood abides in me ('lives in me','is united to me') and I in him" (*John 6:56*).

Abiding in Christ! The most intimate union conceivable between God and man![11] To convey its meaning the Fathers often used the biblical imagery of married love (e.g. *Canticle of Canticles 2:16* : "My beloved is mine and I am his"; the marriage feast at Cana; the parable of the wedding feast, etc.). Beautiful though it be, such imagery must remain inadequate. For here there is union to a degree not known in human love where "two are in one flesh" *(Matthew 19:5)*. Here there is actual *assimilation* (Augustine's phrase, *Confessions 7:10*) of one person into the other, of the believer into Christ.

Paul sees this "abiding" in terms of "putting on" Christ, identifying with Christ, developing within ourselves something of Christ's outlook, attitudes, reactions, commitment to the Father's will; having the mind of Christ: "Let this mind be in you which was in Christ Jesus . . . *(Phil 2:5)*. Holy Communion is the privileged moment of application of this great text. It is the moment above all moments when the Christian must make his own the sentiments which Christ had as he offered himself to the Father in sacrifice—sentiments of praise, thanksgiving, humility, abandonment to the Father's will.[12] It is the moment, in brief, when the Christian pledges himself to accept and to live by the new Covenant, sealed by the blood of Christ.

Perhaps the most valuable commentary on the concept of eucharistic "abiding" in Christ is that given to us by Christ himself in the allegory of the vine *(John 15)*. Unless we abide in Christ, all our efforts are in vain *(v. 4)*. If we abide in him, on the other hand, we will bear much fruit *(v. 5)*. In this way our "abiding" issues in action. It is this which gives glory to the Father *(vv. 5, 7, 8)* with the result *(v. 7)* that whatever we shall ask shall be done for us.

2. Communion, a sharing in the redemptive work of Christ

This follows from the first point. Union implies sharing. When at the Last Supper the apostles partook of the bread and wine over which the blessing had been spoken, they immediately thought in terms of *sharing* in something. In what?

From childhood, they had grown to look on the eating and drinking of the "blessed" bread and wine, at their ritual meals, as a sharing in the blessing pronounced by the head of the table; through eating and drinking they were made recipients of the blessing.[13]

At the Last Supper, however, they were in the presence of something greater by far than the customary "blessing". Jesus had identified the bread and wine with his own self about to be sacrificed. This time their "sharing" was a sharing in Jesus' own redemptive work. "Communion" for the apostles was communion in the sacrifice present before them in the person of Jesus.[14]

So with us. "Communion" is communion with Jesus

risen and living, offering himself to the Father in a timeless, eternal act. It is communion in his redemptive work, his sacrifice, his eternal intercession.

3. Communion, union of Christians with one another

For the apostles, as for orientals even to this day, every banquet presupposed an intimate degree of fellowship, togetherness, brotherliness.[15] Hence, incidentally, the scandal of the Pharisees who protested so vehemently against Jesus' practice of "eating with sinners" *(Luke 15:2)*.

These sentiments of unity reached a heightened degree at the Last Supper through the apostles' common involvement in Christ's work and common commitment to his Covenant. Identifying with Christ, they identified with one another. Jesus urged them on to the ideal degree of unity: "Love one another as I have loved you" *(John 13:34)*, praying to the Father "that they may all be one even as thou art in me and I in thee".

So with us. Because the Eucharist is a sacred banquet it is a *sign* of unity. But more. It effects unity. It gives to the communicant the gift of brotherly love.

For too long this aspect of Communion, and especially its implications for daily living, was overlooked. Hence the repeated pronouncements by the Church, that Communion should have its effect on our daily life, leaving us with an eagerness "to do good, to please God, to live honestly . . . to seek to fill the world with the spirit of Christ" *(EM 13)*. At the level of ritual the Church underlines the same lesson. Hence the kiss of peace, the breaking of bread, the choosing of a communion song which will "express the spiritual communion of the participants and give a fraternal character to the communion procession" *(IG 56i)*.

A final lesson which comes home to us from reflection on this union aspect of Communion: "It is above all in the celebration of the mystery of unity that all Christians should be filled with sorrow at the divisions which separate them" *(EM 8)*. The thought prompts us to pray that God will hasten the day when all will be one, and God will be all in all *(SC 48)*.

Communion under both kinds

The late Archdale A. King in his *Reception of the Chalice: Its Revival* (his last book, which appeared a few days after the esteemed scholar's death in 1972; published by the Liturgy Centre, Carlow College) referred to the reception of the chalice by the laity as "one of the most happy results of the Second Vatican Council" (p. 46). Father Christopher Walsh sees Communion under one kind alone as "an impoverishment of the sacramental sign given to us by our Lord". I quote Father Walsh's crisply written note in full, with the kind permission of the editor of the bulletin of the Shrewsbury Liturgical Commission, where it first appeared:

In Corpus Christi processions we sing the traditional words "Word made flesh, by work he maketh/Very bread his flesh to be;/ Man in wine Christ's blood partaketh . . ." On the eleventh Sunday we have as prayer over the offerings: "O God, you give us bread and wine as our food and drink, and you make them the sacrament which renews our spirit . . ." Such expressions are almost a liturgical commonplace, but for our people mustn't they sound slightly incongruous?

At the Last Supper our Lord gave the Eucharist to his Church in the twofold form of bread and wine, and invited us all to partake in it by eating and drinking: "Take and eat, this is my body . . . Drink this all of you, this is my blood . . ." For 1,200 years all Christians received Communion under both kinds. Eastern Christians, both Catholic and Orthodox, still do, but in the West the practice died out, partly for theological reasons, partly for reasons of convenience. Theologically it was realised that the body and blood of Christ are present whole and entire under either form and that there was therefore no strict need for the laity to receive from the chalice; without it they would not be deprived of any of the sacramental grace, and there would be less danger of accidents. After the Reformation, the Council of Trent considered restoring the tradition but was reluctant to appear to be conceding a point to the Protestants who had already reintroduced it. 400 years later the Second Vatican Council shook off this inhibition and authorised the gradual restoration of the rite *(Constitution on the Liturgy, 55)*. While it is agreed that Communion under either kind is sufficient and that the whole Christ is present under the appearances of either the bread or the wine, it cannot be denied that it constitutes a limitation and an impoverishment of the sacramental sign given to us by our Lord. The sign should be more than just sufficient, it should express symbolically the total meaning and richness of the sacrament.

We have tended, perhaps, to indentify Christ's presence and activity too exclusively with the bread, whereas both bread and wine in complementary ways evoke and symbolise his sacrifice and his presence among us, his presence precisely as food and drink. And in Communion under one kind we do not drink. We do indeed receive Christ's blood, because it is inseparable from his body, but we do not sacramentally drink it. Under both kinds, however, the sign is more expressive, more complete; we make a more perfect memorial of what he did at the Last Supper, we demonstrate more clearly that the Eucharist is a meal, and a festive meal at that, and we associate ourselves more closely with Christ's pouring out his blood for us in the sacrifice of the new covenant (*cf. IG 240*). And in the end, no matter what theological justifications can be elaborated for Communion in one kind, it can hardly be denied that the plain sense of our Lord's words and his obvious intention was that we both eat and drink. Only for the most serious reasons should we continue to modify his instructions. This would seem to indicate that the older tradition should be the normal mode of receiving Communion except in cases of impossibility or serious difficulty. The Church has every intention of making this possible once again. Ever since the Council it has permitted this fuller form of Communion on special occasions like weddings, ordinations, retreats and conferences. Since 1970 it has been left to local bishops to extend this custom.

The rate of advance will obviously depend on pastoral and practical considerations. The larger the congregation the more difficult it will be, without several assistants to help the priest. Larger chalices will eventually have to be found in most parishes, though fifty or more can be communicated from most of our present models. And, most important of all, the entire parish will have to be prepared and instructed in the value and significance of this restoration.

Meanwhile we should be eager to avail of every opportunity we now have, and to stimulate in our people the desire for further opportunities. As their

awareness and appreciation grow, we may antici-
pate further and further extensions until it becomes
once more a universal custom. Then we will be able
to use the third of the eucharistic acclamations
without self-consciousness or incongruity:

When we eat this bread and drink this cup,
we proclaim your death, Lord Jesus,
until you come in glory.

Cleansing of the sacred vessels

When the distribution of holy Communion is over,
the priest may gather up any fragments and, at the side
of the altar, cleanse the sacred vessels. The vessels are
then removed by the server to the credence table.

A better practice, it would appear, and one which
the rubrics also permit, is for the priest to cleanse the
sacred vessels when Mass is over, and the assembly
dismissed. In this way the rather ungracious-looking
gesticulations to which the faithful are sometimes
subjected, and which they find so tedious and distracting,
are avoided.

After Communion

"Priest and people may pray in their hearts for
some time. A hymn or some other canticle of praise may
be sung (or said) by all" *(IG 56j)*. Here again variety is
important. A well-intentioned celebrant could easily
find himself devoting this interval after communion to
leading the people in prayer, thus witholding from them
an opportunity for the silent communal prayer envisaged
by the missal.

Post Communion

The celebrant prays for the fruits of the mystery which has been celebrated. The short conclusion "through Christ our Lord" is used.

Announcements

At this point announcements, if there are any, are made. With pastoral concern the missal says that such announcements are to be brief. At this point too the celebrant may say his own final word of dismissal to the people.

Blessing

The greeting and final blessing follow. As an enriching surround, the missal provides variable "prayers over the people". The "Go forth in peace" is reminiscent of Christ's great "Go . . . teach all nations" of the Gospel. It is the solemn sending forth of the assembly to carry the Christian message to the world, and to make their lives a continual "eucharist" or thanksgiving under the guidance of the Holy Spirit.

6 Group Masses

Pastoral value

Experience is bearing out the value of the small group Mass. The fact that the participants can easily see the altar and hear the Word, that functions are widely shared, that participants may be of the same age, may be members of the same organisation, may share the same apostolate—all these can help to achieve a degree of communal participation not possible in the larger assembly.

The Church has officially recognised the pastoral value of group celebration.[1] An Instruction of the Congregation for Divine Worship, 15 May 1969, speaks of the value of such celebrations "in meeting special needs and deepening the Christian life according to the requirements and the preparation of the participants. If they are well directed", the document continues, "such celebrations, instead of damaging the unity of the parish, actually benefit its missionary activity by bringing people closer together and deepening the formation of others." A note issued by the French episcopal liturgical commission in February 1970 says that group Masses "can deepen the Christian life of the participants, integrate them more effectively into the Church, and increase their apostolic involvement". The Benedictines of Ampleforth, in a recent study of the question, point to "the real sense of church which the participants

experience, of relatedness to God in each other . . .".
Behind these observations is the finding of psycho-
sociological studies that it is at the level of the small
group within a wider group that one best discovers one's
sense of belonging to the wider group.

Dangers

A certain caution is required, however, in the
handling of group celebrations. Such celebrations can be
a tempting occasion for the introduction of the bizarre.
The bizarre can be alluring; but it can also be bewilder-
ing even to the extent of leaving the participants uneasy
in their faith. Here the celebrant must guard particularly
against any tendency to impose his own subjective view
of worship on the people. The people of God have the
right of access to the Church's entire treasury of worship
and prayer. It is not for the priest to set himself up as a
dispenser of what he personally feels is good for the
people. He is the dispenser of the authentic worship of
the Church. It is through his concern for authenticity in
worship that the priest proves his fidelity to liturgical
law in the best sense of that expression.[2]
Another danger with the group Mass is the danger
of fragmentation. A group Mass must never result in the
creation of an inward-looking élite, or in prejudicing the
participants against the Sunday assembly. The group
must remain ecclesial, catholic, in its thinking and in its
celebration—for example, in the bidding prayers, which
must be orientated towards the universal needs of the
Church. In the group Mass, no less than in the larger
assembly, it is the entire Church which is offering the
Eucharist, and the entire Church which is being offered.
"The Christian assembly", I wrote elsewhere, "is one.
It does not cater for cliques. The ideal Eucharist is that

which gathers together the faithful of every age and kind and walk of life. In the eucharistic assembly all must feel at home—black and white, rich and poor, adult and teenager. Any suggestion of social distinction in our assemblies draws from us an indignant reaction. But distinctions are equally reprehensible when made on the basis of age or mentality. All must feel at home in their Father's house. All must feel welcome—Jew and Greek, slave and free, male and female, young and old *(Gal 3:28)*. All are one in Christ Jesus."[3]

Integrating personal prayer into the group celebration

We are all familiar with the growing Pentecostal spirituality in the world today, and with group-prayer or shared-prayer trends, where members of a group come together to pray in a spontaneous, uninhibited fashion. It would seem to be desirable to integrate this kind of prayer into the small-group Eucharist. I have experienced this form of celebration with different types of groups—priests, seminarians, teenagers, religious. Praying was "shared" at three points: after the examination of conscience, when members of the group spontaneously confessed their failings aloud (obviously in a general fashion); after the homily, when members shared their reactions to the Word; and, finally, after communion. Here once more the power of the "shared experience" in the liturgy was evident.[4] But again, a word of warning. The art of formulating prayer comes hard. We are not born with the gift of spontaneous charismatic intervention. People who seem gifted in this respect are people who have thought prayerfully and deeply beforehand on what they have to say. If on the other hand, someone with an impoverished spiritual background assumes to intervene spontaneously at prayer, the result can reflect a poverty of content and hesitancy of expression which will bore the listeners to the point of irritation.

7 Mass on Special Occasions

The gamut of "special occasion" Masses seems endless. One could attempt a classification on the basis of setting, choice of celebrant, liturgical time, etc. Thus a Mass may be "special" because the celebrant is newly ordained, or a jubilarian; or because of the time of year—Christmas, Ash Wednesday; or because of a particular sacrament or liturgical function associated with the celebration (a wedding, a funeral); or because there is something special about the setting (a classroom, a boy-scout camp, a battlefield). One would need the vision of a Malachi to scan the range of possibilities.

This chapter proffers some suggestions which are particularly applicable to the "special occasion" Mass, and which may help towards harnessing these valuable pastoral moments to best possible effect.

Principle of sensitiveness to the congregation's heightened level of awareness

One finds this principle written into all post-Vatican II liturgical documentation from the magisterium. If the principle was neglected in the past it was because the thrust of celebration was on the sanctuary. The celebrant was the faceless performer of ritual, carrying out stupendous work, oblivious, it appeared, of the silent onlookers. The new Roman Missal puts the spotlight once more, as in the early Church, on the congregation: "The Lord's Supper is the assembly of the people of God who come together to celebrate the memorial of the Lord, under the presidency of a priest . . ." So the *Institutio Generalis* (first edition) describes the Mass.[1] Here we see that it is not the priest alone who celebrates the Eucharist. The assembly celebrates. The Eucharist belongs to the assembly. The priest is the servant of the assembly. He must defer to it, be sensitive to it.

Hence the new Missal bids the celebrant to celebrate not merely in accordance with the rubrics, but in such a way as to convey the meaning of the sacred actions.[2] Nor may he impose his own idiosyncrasies on the people; he must consider their common spiritual good rather than his own preferences.

This sensitiveness on the part of the celebrant is spelled out with painstaking detail in the new rite of funerals. There the priest is told to show "loving concern" for the mourners, to "support them in their sorrow", to "lighten their burden", to "strengthen their hope", to "foster their faith".[3] He is to defer to the wishes of the family in making the funeral arrangements, and to involve them in the planning of the liturgy. He is to be especially aware of any lukewarm or *lapsi* who happen to be present.

The findings of modern psychology bear out the value of this celebration-sensitiveness. Psychologists[4] speak of the range of levels of awareness at which the mind functions, from the "dulled" to the "heightened" level. Applying this to the eucharistic assembly, they would see the average Sunday congregation as functioning at a "dulled" level of awareness—a home truth which will scarcely cause clerical eyebrows to rise in surprise! Such a congregation is not particularly receptive, not particularly impressionable.

On the other hand, participants at a special-occasion Mass are at a heightened level of awareness. They are at a "crisis-point"—not in the sensational or derogatory sense of the expression, but in the sense that they are questioning. At a funeral Mass, for example, people are questioning the nature of the hereafter. They are watching the reactions of the bereaved, questioning the goodness of God who has permitted perhaps the sudden death of a young husband or an expectant mother.

Often this will be the *kairós*, the hour of grace, for someone in that congregation, the hour of the Lord's passing *(Exodus 12:11)*, the moment of "decisive experience"[5] as Archbishop Anthony Bloom puts it. The sensitive celebrant must ask: how can such a situation be most effectively handled?

Our renewed liturgical practice points to the answer, in the distribution of functions during the celebration: "Each person should perform his own function, doing all that the nature of the liturgy requires of him, and only that" *(SC 28)*. Reading, carrying the gifts, proclaiming the intentions at the bidding prayers— these functions belong to the laity, and are not to be swallowed up by the celebrant.

Here again, psychology bears out the wisdom of the Church's practice. A person at a "special-occasion" Mass may be more influenced through the sharing of a crisis moment with another member of the congregation than by anything the celebrant can say or do. An incident will illustrate the point. A young girl whom I knew died. She was twenty-three. The most moving moment of the funeral Mass was when her young brother read the scripture passage. His bearing, his sincerity, his manner of performing his function, all bore witness to his acceptance of God's will and his belief in a life to come. Similarly at a wedding. For example: a young husband's request, in the bidding prayers, that God may "bless our marriage and the marriage of all newly-weds" can bear stronger witness to the Church's conviction in respect of the marriage contract, than any word from the celebrant. I began by saying that the gamut of special-occasion Masses is vast. It ranges over "every conceivable human circumstance from the pinnacles of earthly greatness to the refuge of fugitives in the caves and dens of the earth". The citation is from the late Gregory Dix's *The Shape of the Liturgy*. The author is commenting on our Lord's command to "do this as an anamnesis of me". He continues in a passage of beautiful lyricism which I append as a conclusion to this chapter.

> Men have found no better thing than this to do for kings at their crowning and for criminals going to the scaffold; for armies in triumph or for a bride and bridegroom in a little country church; for the proclamation of a dogma or for a good crop of wheat; for the wisdom of the parliament of a mighty nation or for a sick old woman afraid to die; for a schoolboy sitting an examination or for Columbus setting out to discover America; for the famine of whole provinces or for the soul of a dead lover; in thankfulness because my father did not die of pneumonia; for a village headman much tempted to return to fetish because the yams had failed; because the Turk was at the gates of Vienna; for the repentance of Margaret; for the settlement of a strike; for the son of a barren woman; for Captain so-and-so, wounded and prisoner of war; while the lions roared in the nearby amphitheatre; on the beach at Dunkirk; while the hiss of scythes in the thick June grass came faintly through the windows of the church; tremulously, by an old monk on the fiftieth anniversary of his vows; furtively, by an

exiled bishop who had hewn timber all day in a prison camp near Murmansk; gorgeously, for the canonisation of St Joan of Arc—one could fill many pages with the reasons why men have done this, and not tell a hundredth part of them. And best of all, week by week, and month by month, on a hundred thousand successive Sundays, faithfully. unfailingly, across all the parishes of Christendom, the pastors have done this just to make the plebs sancta Dei—the holy common people of God.[6]

8   A Sacral Setting for Celebration

A few years ago it was commonplace to hear of certain extravagant attempts to desacrilise the eucharistic celebration. One heard of celebrants clad in jeans and T-shirts, using plastic beakers for chalices, beach tables for altars, and loaves of bread direct from the food-market.

The desacrilisation debate is one of the big questions facing the Church in the late twentieth century. Briefly it can be put as follows. According to the "desacrilisers" nothing is profane; everything in the world, sin alone excepted, has been made holy by the incarnation. Applying this to the liturgy, the exponents of desacrilisation maintain that the setting aside of vessels, vestments, buildings and the like for divine worship is not only unnecessary; it is a form of holy play-acting which is a betrayal of the Gospel.

The arguments from the other side are fairly summed up in a remark of Hugh Montefiore: "We need symbols of the sacred in the midst of the secular to remind us that all is sacred."[1] With this view I am in sympathy. We are not mere rational beings. We have bodies. To reduce worship to something purely interior would be to go against the nature of man, to go against the incarnation. True, God is not confined to sacred buildings, but, as John Maquarrie argues,[2] if there are no such focal points where we can become sensitive to

God's presence, then we risk failing altogether to recognise that presence in the broad undistinguished stretches of the world. We need the sacred oasis in the secular desert.

Father Congar calls this the "pedagogical sacred",[3] the setting apart of certain words, gestures, vestments, places and times to help promote our communion with the divinity. It is something merely functional, he says, involving no depreciation of the profane.

We must therefore sacrilise. We need sacred signs to lift us up out of our daily humdrum existence, to remind us of the transcendent, of a world other than the present one. As Tillich puts it: "Sacred places, sacred times, sacred acts are necessary to counter-balance the profane which tends to cut us off from our relation with the ultimate good, the source of our being, and which tends to conceal our experience of the sacred beneath the dust of daily living."[4]

And yet one sympathises readily with the exponents of desacrilisation, for often they are reacting against— and thereby draw our attention to—certain regrettable features of our liturgy. Two in particular may be singled out for attention:

a. The "aseptic" in the liturgy, by which I mean the off-putting, the unreal. One thinks in this connection of vestments, for instance, of the kind which do justice neither to the humanity nor the masculinity of the priest;[5] altar appointments, tasteless to the point of nausea; breads of that papery, unbreadlike quality implicitly condemned in the new Missal; altars of the kind described in one issue of *Worship* as "theological and aesthetic monstrosities"[6]; churches, tawdry in design to the point of trumpery. One recalls Vatican II's broadside against "works of art which are repugnant to faith, morals and Christian piety, and which offend the true religious sense either by depraved forms or through lack of artistic merit".[7]

b. The divorce of liturgy from life is the other concern of the desacrilisers, as it is ours. Here, however, let me say at once that we are not going to wed liturgy to life by hackneying the liturgy, by reducing worship to the commonplace. We relate liturgy to life, by ensuring the internal participation of the worshippers, by leading them, for example, through the experience of deep reflection on the Word (asking themselves: What is God saying to me? How does this word apply to my life now, tomorrow . . .?); by leading them to commit themselves, pledge themselves, anew, to the new covenant. Worship will be genuinely related to life to the extent that the worshippers are renewed in their faith, their love, their com-union:

Communion

> Com-union!
> The word rings out the Christian ideal.
> A Church at one
> a world at one
> man one with man
> man one with his God
> man, through the Spirit,
> one with the Father
> one with the Son.
>
> In
>   the Mass
> is this Communion
>   celebrated
>   signified
>   effected.

Therefore
    is the Mass
both
       summit and source
       of all Christian activity.

For this, the Mass, was
       the world created
       the Church founded
       the Word made flesh.

So that
       at the heart of the Church
       at the heart of the world
       at the heart of the Divine Plan
is
the MASS.

Notes

1 Opening Rites of Mass

1. *Directory for Children's Masses*, S.C.D.W., 1 November 1973.
2. IG 7.
3. *Roman Missal*, 82.
4. *Building and Reorganisation of Churches*, Pastoral Directory of the Episcopal Liturgical Commission of Ireland, Veritas, 1972.
5. May be used at any Mass. IG 235.
6. A. G. MARTIMORT, *The Church at Prayer* (Irish University Press, 1968), p. 161.
7. MARTIMORT, op. cit., p. 164.
8. MARUCCHI, *The Catholic Encyclopaedia*, vol. 4 (Caxton, 1908), pp. 526 ff.
9. NOELLE MAURICE DENIS-BOULET in *La Maison Dieu*, 75, pp. 66–67.
10. An interesting specimen of processional cross is the twelfth century cross of Cong, one of the great art treasures of Ireland, now in the National Museum. The cross is of oak, covered with copper plates with gold filigree decoration. The cross was made in 1123 for the High King of Ireland, Turlough More O'Conor, from whom the Reverend Charles O'Connor, S.J., is twenty-fourth in descent.
11. 1st April, 1970.
12. See EDMUND JONES, OSB, in *Life and Worship*, no. 174.
13. E. GERSON-KIWI, art. "Musique" in *Dictionnaire de la Bible Supplément*, vol. 5, col. 1436.
14. According to the new legislation, in the Roman Missal, a fixed altar is consecrated. Hence it does not require an altar stone. A movable altar is either consecrated or blessed. There is no obligation to place an altar stone on a movable altar or on a table which is used for Mass outside a holy place, church, oratory, etc. (IG 265, 260). However, if an altar which has not

been consecrated or blessed is used regularly in a church or oratory, it would seem advisable to use an altar stone on it until it is consecrated or blessed.

15. The very design of the altar should help inspire reverence. Many so-called "temporary altars" offend in this respect. In any case "temporary arrangements of churches should gradually be given a final form. Some provisory solutions, already reproved by the *Consilium*, are still in use, although they are liturgically and artistically unsatisfactory, and render difficult the worthy celebration of Mass." (S.C.D.W., 5 Sept. 1970).

16. J. D. CRICHTON, *Christian Celebration: The Mass* (G. Chapman, 1971), pp. 69 f.

17. MARTIMORT, op. cit., p. 82.

18. Text referred to by L. Deiss in his admirable *Spirit and Song of the New Liturgy* (World Library of Sacred Music, 1970), p. 121.

19. DEISS, op. cit., p. 122.

20. For the commentary on the greetings I am indebted to Peter Dacquino, *"I Saluti Liturgici nel Nuovo Rito Della Missa"* in Notitiae, 55, pp. 254 f.; McKenzie, *Dictionary of the Bible* (Chapman 1965); and Father Cyril Clarke, C.P.

21. OSCAR CULLMAN, *Early Christian Worship* (SCM Press, 1966), p. 24.

22. As it is today for Jews (shalom) and Moslems (salaam).

23. Op. cit., p. 652.

24. EM 20.

25. See EP, Letter of Congr. of Divine Worship to presidents of episcopal conferences, 27 April 1973.

26. EP 27 April 1973.

27. *Musicam Sacram* (1967), par. 10.

28. *Osservatore Romano* (28 May 1970).

29. A point made by Father Jeremiah Threadgold at a liturgy congress in Droichead Nua, December 1971.

30. DEISS, *Spirit and Song of the New Liturgy*, World Library of Sacred Music, p. 193.

31. *L'Église en Prière* (Desclée, 1965), p. 344.

32. DEISS, op. cit., p. 190.

33. *Before Mass*, Longman, Green and Co. Ltd, 1957.

2 Liturgy of the Word

1. SC 51, 52.

2. SC 43.

3. SC 7.

4. The presence of Christ in the Eucharist is a real presence *speciali modo* (EM 9).
5. *In Joannem*, 30.1.
6. E.g. Origen: Henry Bettenson, *The Early Christian Fathers*, Oxford University Press, 1956, p. 344. *Hom. in Exod.*, XIII, 3.
7. EM 10.
8. "An invitation drawing us and moving us to believe". St Thomas as quoted by Father Schillebeeckx in *Parole et Sacrament* in *Lumière et Vie*, 46 (1960), p. 36.
9. Pastoral directory of Irish Episcopal Liturgical Commission, on *Building and Reorganisation of Churches*.
10. IG 41.
11. At the Liturgy Seminar, Carlow, 9–10 May 1972.
12. FATHER LUCIEN DEISS at the Liturgy Seminar, Carlow, May 1972.
13. CLARKE and JASPER, *Initiation and Eucharist* (London, SPCK, 1972), pp. 29–30. One finds certain reservations too in Deiss, *Spirit and Song of the New Liturgy* (World Library of Sacred Music, 1970), and Gelineau, *Dans Vos Assemblées* (Desclée, 1971).
14. CHAPMAN, London, 1971. This and Father Deiss's *Spirit and Song of the New Liturgy* are the best books in English that have come to my notice on the subject of the celebration of the Eucharist.
15. CHAPMAN LTD.
16. CLARKE and JASPER, op. cit., p. 24.
17. DEISS, *Spirit and Song*, p. 166.

3 Preparation of the Gifts

1. *Osservatore Romano*, French ed., 23 May 1969, p. 2.
2. JUNGMANN, *Missarum Sollemnia*, vol. 2, p. 307 (Aubier, 1958).
3. *Didaché*, 9, written c. 100 A.D. See also, for example, the fourth-century anaphora of Serapion where the idea recurs.
4. JEREMIAS, *The Eucharistic Words of Jesus* (SCM Press, 1966), p. 223.
5. *Building and Reorganisation of Churches* (Veritas, 1973), p. 42.
6. CYPRIAN, P. L., 4, col. 612–13.
7. See, e.g., *Hippolytus, Apostolic Tradition*, ed. Botte (Aschendorfische Verlagsbuchhandlung, Münster, Westfalen, 1963).
8. DEISS, *Spirit and Song of the New Liturgy* (World Library of Sacred Music, 1970), p. 141.
9. See USA Bishops' Commission on the Liturgy, 1968 statement.
10. CYPRIAN, Letter 63 to Caecelia.
11. DIX, *The Shape of the Liturgy* (Dacre Press, 1964), p. 124.

4   Liturgy of the Eucharist

1. IG 54.
2. MAX THURIAN, *The Eucharistic Memorial*, part 2, page 44. Lutterworth Press, 1961.
3. IG 54.
4. HIPPOLYTUS, *Apostolic Tradition*.
5. See Byzantine and Armenian rites.
6. This is the interpretation which appeals most to me among the various explanations offered by scholars such as Jungmann, Dekkers, N. M. Denis-Boulet, Bouyer.
7. *La Maison Dieu*, 87, p. 107.
8. MARTIMORT, *The Church at Prayer: the Eucharist*, Irish University Press, 1973.
9. DEISS: *Spirit and Song of the New Liturgy*, World Library of Sacred Music, 1970, pp. 81, 90.
10. See Martimort, op. cit., p. 155; Thurian, op. cit., pp. 35, 44. McGoldrick, *Understanding the Eucharist*, Gill, 1969, p. 32 (an article which I have found extremely helpful in the preparation of the present commentary); Crichton, *Christian Celebration: The Mass*, Chapman 1971, p. 48.
11. For a study of this concept see especially Jeremias, *The Eucharistic Words of Jesus*, SCM Press 1966, and Thurian, op. cit.
12. On the importance of singing at these moments (even in preference to entrance, offertory, communion and recession), see *Musicam Sacram*, 1967, Instruction of the Congr. of Rites on music in the liturgy.
13. See letter of Congr. of Divine Worship to presidents of episcopal conferences, 27 April 1973.

5   Communion

1. C.D.W., *Eucharistiae Participationem*, 27 April 1973.
2. *La Maison Dieu*, 74, p. 85.
3. OSCAR CULLMANN, *Early Christian Worship*, SCM Press, 1966, pp. 12f.
4. JOACHIM JEREMIAS, *The Lord's Prayer*, Facet Books, 1964, p. 23f.
5. MAX THURIAN, *Eucharist*, Faith Press, 1962, p. 21.
6. DUFOUR, *Vocabulary of Biblical Theology*; MCKENZIE, *Dictionary of the Bible*, Chapman Ltd.
7. A reference mentioned by Father Crichton in *Christian Celebration*, p. 99.

8. *Serm.* 227.
9. *Newsletter*, vol. 7, 1972 reproduced in *Notitiae*, April 1973.
10. A story is told of the late English scholar Archdale A. King, who did not take easily to some of the post-Vatican II changes in the liturgy, that once at Mass when approached by an Italian lady in his pew at the kiss of peace he replied: "Good heavens, Madame, no, please, not here in church!"
11. C. H. DODD, *The Interpretation of the Fourth Gospel*, Cambridge University Press, 1968, p. 197.
12. MARMION, *Christ the Life of the Soul*, Sands, p. 272; *Mediator Dei*, London CTS, 1947, par. 85.
13. JOACHIM JEREMIAS, *The Eucharistic Words of Jesus*, SCM Press, 1964, 204f, 232f. *Eucharisticum Mysterium*, 1967, 3b. *Mediator Dei*, cit. 85.
14. JOSEPH POWERS, *Eucharistic Theology*, B. and O., Herder, 1968, 54, 57, 68–9. MAX THURIAN, *The Eucharistic Memorial*, II, Lutterworth Press, 1965, 103.
15. JOACHIM JEREMIAS, *op. cit.*

6   Group Masses

1. Since this chapter was written the Dublin Liturgical Commission has published a useful booklet on *The Small-Group Mass*, price 25p. See also an excellent article by Brian Gogan in *The Furrow*, March 1974.
2. See Instruction of 5 September 1970, Congregation of Divine Worship which says : "A priest by imposing his own personal restoration of sacred rites offends against the rights of the faithful, and introduces individualism and idiosyncrasy into celebrations which belong to the whole Church."
3. New Liturgy, no. 15 (Carlow College), p. 2.
4. See chapter 7 "Mass on Special Occasions" p. 85.

7   Mass on Special Occasions

1. *Institutio Generalis*, art. 7. Following Fr Crichton (op. cit., p. 51ff) I prefer the unrevised text.
2. Op. cit., arts. 313, 316.
3. *Praenotanda* of the *Ordo Exsequiarum*, 1969.
4. On this point, I am indebted to Miss Nuala McDonald, lecturer in Galway University.
5. *School for Prayer*, Darton, Longman and Todd, 1970, p. 51.
6. Dacre Press, 1964, p. 744.

8 A Sacral Setting for Celebration

1. MONTEFIORE, *Can Man Survive?* (Collins, 1970), p. 134.
2. *Paths in Spirituality*, SCM, 1972, p. 84.
3. CONGAR, *La Liturgie après Vatican II*, Cerf, 1967, p. 399.
4. *La Maison Dieu*, no. 96. *Honneté et Sens du Sacre*, p. 14.
5. Anyone who has seen *Fellini Roma* will recall how effectively and how nastily that film jibes at so-called "ecclesiastical" vestments.
6. *Worship*, 44–5, p. 295.
7. SC 124.

Bibliography

Prime Sources with abbreviations used in text

SC: *Sacrosanctum Concilium,* Constitution on the Liturgy, 4 December 1963.

SL: *Sacram Liturgiam,* Motu Proprio of Paul VI, 25 January 1964.

IO: *Inter Oecumenici,* On Implementing the Liturgy, S.C.R., 26 September 1964.

Decretum Generale: Concelebration and Communion under both Species, S.C.R., 7 March 1965.

SM: *Musicam Sacram,* On Sacred Music, S.C.R., 5 March 1967.

Tres Abhinc Annos, On Further Implementation of the Liturgy, S.C.R., 4 May 1967.

EM: Eucharisticum Mysterium, On the Worship of the Eucharistic Mystery, S.C.R., 25 May 1967

IG: *General Instruction on the Roman Missal,* S.C.D.W., 26 March 1970.

MQ: *Ministerium Quaedam,* Motu Proprio of Paul VI, 15 August 1972.

IC: *Immensae Caritatis,* Instruction of S.C. Sacraments, 29 January 1973.

EP: *Eucharistiae Participationem,* On the Eucharistic Prayers, S.C.D.W., 27 April 1973.

De Sacra Communione et de Cultu Mysterii Eucharistici extra Missam, S.C.D.W., 21 June 1973.

Directory on Children's Masses, S.C.D.W., 1 November 1973.

Eucharistic Theology and History

BOUYER, L., *The Eucharist,* University of Notre Dame Press, 1966.

DE BACIOCCHI, *L'Eucharistie,* Desclée, 1961.

CULLMANN, O., *Early Christian Worship,* SCM Press, London, 1953.

DIX, G., *The Shape of the Liturgy,* Dacre Press, London, 1945.

HAMMAN, A., *The Mass: Ancient Liturgies and Patristic Texts*, Alba House, New York, 1968.

HURLEY, M., *Church and Eucharist*, Gill, Dublin, 1966.

JEREMIAS, J., *The Eucharistic Words of Jesus*, SCM Press, London, 1966.

JUNGMANN, J., *Missarum Sollemnia, The Mass of the Roman Rite*, Benziger Brothers, New York, 1951.

LASH, N., *His Presence in the World, A Study of Eucharistic Worship and Theology*, Sheed and Ward: London and Sydney, 1968.

MCGOLDRICK, P., *Understanding the Eucharist*, Gill and Macmillan, Dublin, 1969.

MARTIMORT, A. G., *The Church at Prayer: The Eucharist*, Irish University Press, 1973.

MAURICE-DENIS, N., and BOULET, ROBERT, *Eucharistie*, Letouzey et Ané, Paris, 1953.

POWERS, J. M., *Eucharistic Theology*, Burns and Oates, London, 1968.

SCHILLEBEECKX, E., *The Eucharist*, Sheed and Ward, London and Sydney, 1968.

SHEPPARD, L., (ed.), *The New Liturgy*, Darton, Longman and Todd, London, 1970.

THURIAN, M., *The Eucharistic Memorial*, 2 volumes, Lutterworth Press, London, 1960–1.

Eucharistic Celebration

CHAMPLIN, J., *The Priest and God's People at Prayer*, Chapman, London, 1971.

CLARKE, RAYMOND, *Sounds Effective*, Chapman, London, Dublin, Melbourne, 1969.

COUGHLAN, P. *The New Mass, A Pastoral Guide*, Chapman, London, Dublin, Melbourne, 1969.

CRICHTON, J.D., *Christian Celebration: The Mass*, Chapman, London, 1971.

DEISS, L., *Spirit and Song of the New Liturgy*, World Library of Sacred Music, 1970.

GELINEAU, J., *Dans Vos Assemblées*, 2 volumes, Desclée, 1970.

GUARDINI, R., *Before Mass*, Longman, Green and Co., Ltd., 1957.

MANLEY, GREGORY, *At the Table of the Lord*, Victoria, 1972.

MARTIMORT, A. G., *op. cit.*, in previous section.

ROGUET, A. M., *The New Mass*, Catholic Book Publishing Co., New York, 1970.

THURIAN, M., *The Eucharistic Liturgy of Taizé*, The Faith Press, Leighton, 1962.

Liturgy of the Word

In addition to the works listed above:

BAILLARGEON, A., *New Media, New Forms*, Catholic Homiletic Society, 1967.

CRICHTON, J. D. and others, *The Mass and the People of God*, Burns and Oates, London, 1966.

JUNGMANN, J., *The Liturgy of the Word*, Burns and Oates, London, 1966.

MILNER, P. and others, *The Ministry of the Word*, Liturgical Press, Collegeville, 1967.

MARTIMORT, A. G. and others, *The Liturgy of the Word*, Liturgical Press, Collegeville, 1959.

Holy Communion

In addition to the works listed above:

DODD, C. H., *The Interpretation of the Fourth Gospel*, Cambridge University Press, 1968.

FEUILLET, A., *Le Discours sur le Pain de Vie*, Desclée, 1967.

FEUILLET, A., *Retraite Eucharistique*, Rhodanique S.A., Switzerland.

SCHURMANN, H., *Le Récit de la Dernière Cène*, Xavier Mappus, Le Puy, 1965.

Eastern Rites

CABASILAS, N., *Commentary on the Divine Liturgy*, SPCK, London, 1960.

DALMAIS, I., *The Eastern Liturgies*, Hawthorne Books, New York, 1960.

DICK, I., *Qu'est-ce que l'Orient Chretien*, Casterman, 1965.

Petit Paroissien des Liturgies Orientales, St Paul, Harissa, 1941.

Church Building

Building and Reorganisation of Churches, Pastoral Directory of the Episcopal Liturgical Commission of Ireland, Veritas, 1973.

Periodicals

Assemblée Nouvelle, 1 rue de l'Abbé Grégoire, Paris 6.
Église qui Chante, 31 rue de Fleurus, Paris 6.
La Maison Dieu, 29 bvd. Latour Maubourg, Paris 7.
Life and Worship, Fowler Wright Books, Tenbury Wells, Worcs.
New Liturgy, Mount St Anne's Liturgy Centre, Portarlington, Ireland.
Notitiae, Libreria Editrice Vaticana, Rome.
Worship, St John's Abbey, Collegeville, Minnesota 56321.